MW00774066

OVERCOMERS

OVERCOMERS

How to Change Your Life in 31 Days!

DONNELL S. JOSIAH, PHD, PMP

Overcomers: How to Change Your Life in 31 Days!
by Donnell S. Josiah, PhD, PMP

Cover Design by Henry McEachnie of Graphic Eye Designs.

© Copyright 2015

SAINT PAUL PRESS, DALLAS, TEXAS

First Printing, 2015

All rights reserved. No part of this publication may be reproduced, stored in a retrieval system, or transmitted in any form or by any means, electronic, mechanical, photocopying, recording, or otherwise, without the prior permission of the copyright owner, except for brief quotations included in a review of the book.

ISBN-10: 0-9963241-6-X
ISBN-13: 978-0-9963241-6-8

Printed in the U.S.A.

Endorsements

"Impactful, innovative, engaging, and empowering are the words that come to mind after reading *Overcomers*. Dr. Donnell Josiah eloquently puts into words life principles and personal development strategies that not only helped him overcome many obstacles, but also provides a repeatable roadmap for others to do the same. I have personally witnessed how Dr. Josiah immediately put these principles into action when we faced some extremely difficult challenges in our business. The impact was immediate and helped turn what was a set-back into a notable business success story. He has a tenacious drive for excellence, an unwavering commitment to hard work, and an evangelical passion for making a difference in the lives of those he comes in contact with. As his business mentor, I am extremely proud of his accomplishments, not only as a thought leader in the business world, but also as a musician, artist, husband, father, and now author. Dr. Josiah is a true renaissance man who is destined to change the world. I have no doubt that his book *Overcomers* will awaken your personal purpose with passion and conviction, so that you can achieve your God-given destiny and in the process enhance the quality of life for all humanity."

Robert L. Wallace
President and CEO of BITHGROUP Technologies, Inc.
Author of: *Strategic Partnerships: An Entrepreneur's Guide To Joint Ventures And Alliances, Black Wealth and Black Wealth through Black Entrepreneurship, Soul Food, Strategic Partnerships, The Ssese Principles, Green Gold, Crash, The Color of A Billion*

"Donnell Josiah in his first book knocks the proverbial ball out the park. He certainly joins the ranks of the others who have written on the subject of personal development, but there is something distinctly different here; He does not write from dry theory, but he has experienced first-hand everything he writes on these pages. I was most affected by the section on discipline, as I have had a front row seat in watching Donnell succeed against all odds using sustained disciplined deployed over the long haul. But what most sets this book apart, is Donnell's unabashed recognition that without God, none of this works, but with God, your life can change—indeed!"

Frederick Russell
Senior Pastor, Barean SDA Church, Atlanta, GA
Former President, Allegheny West Conference of Seventh Day Adventists

"In *Overcomers*, Donnell Josiah speaks the language of the secular from the vantage point and heart of the sacred. This book is practical. It's packed not with problems, but solutions. It's for parents, professionals, and anyone trying to take their life and career to the 'next' level. I loved it. In our instantaneous culture, we want short cuts and easy solutions. There are none. Biblical principles do however, produce results. Years ago, I told Dr. Josiah, he was a freak of nature. He has the creativity of an artist and the task orientation of a bureaucrat. Those two personality traits should not exist in one frame! But they do. So, as an 'overcomer' Donnell shares overcoming principles. In his latest offering, the table is spread. As I lick my fingers, I encourage you to "Go feast!""

Rev. Dr. Edward P. Harding Jr.
Director of Field Education,
Howard University School of Divinity in Washington, DC.
Senior Pastor, Prince George's Community Presbyterian Church,
Springdale, MD.

"Electrifying, energizing, emancipating. These are the words I would use to describe this book written by a man whom God himself has ordained to travel a specific path so that his story could inspire others to believe against all odds. If you have ever faced fears, self doubt, critics, whose words dampened your spirit and demolished your aspirations, Donnell Josiah's real life journey and practical insights will recharge your vision, reignite your hopes, and restore your dreams."

Dr. ET Stoddart
Senior Pastor, Church of The Oranges SDA Church
City of Orange, NJ

"*Overcomers* is a flood of courageous reflection that can help unlock anyone's personal potential.Donnell Josiah transparently digs into the journey of his life to extract the key principles that have propelled him from an academic failure to a man that holds a PhD and runs three successful businesses. Each daily motivational reading breezes seamlessly from storytelling to battle-tested concepts that are ready for application into everyday life. A refreshing read that empowers and equips you to overcome your most formidable struggles and fulfill your greatest dreams."

David Franklin
Senior Pastor, Miracle Temple SDA Church
Baltimore, MD

Contents

Acknowledgments

When I reflect over my life and recount the many bumps, bruises, but also the many victories, I am grateful for the individuals who have walked with me, encouraged me, and sometimes challenged me to reach for the stars. Just over 40 years ago, two parents welcomed me into this world and surrounded me with siblings that provided a safe haven for my development. To Lennie, Pearline, Lenard and Lenore, I say thank you for your unending love, support, and encouragement through the years. Now as an adult, I am even more grateful for my own family that has provided me with many laughs and countless memories, and who has supported me in each and every endeavor. To my wife Denise, thank you for encouraging me, pushing me, challenging me, and standing with me through so many ups and downs. You are the reason why I exist, why I love, and why I pursue excellence each and every day. To my sons Darryl and Derwen, always remember that the path to your prize is through perseverance. I challenge you to push through the limits and pursue your dreams. To my extended family, a host of colleagues and friends in DMV, and countless others scattered across the United States, thank you for supporting my vision and for investing your time and resources to make *Overcomers* a reality. From the bottom of my heart, thank you!

Tribute

She was a short and stately lady who was not afraid to confront her obstacles. She was passionate about excellence and the pursuit of it. She exercised discipline with a firm hand and loved with abundant grace. She etched in the minds of her children the notion that anything is possible if you are willing to work hard. She inspired the best in us and challenged us to become go-getters. My story would not be the same without her. My success could not have been achieved without her. My first book would not be complete without acknowledgment of her. While my inspiration, my joy, my friend, my Mom is not here in person to witness the culmination of her own labor, I am honored to dedicate this book, *Overcomers: How To Change Your Life In 31 Days*, in tribute to the legacy and memory of my hero, my mom, Pearline Agatha Williams-Josiah.

Introduction

Who would have thought that I would have time to write a 31-day motivational book that helps everyday people achieve extraordinary success? Certainly not me! Why even undertake such a time-consuming and mentally draining project given my already hectic lifestyle? I'll tell you why: Every day, millions of people wake up to confront the same giants that defeated them yesterday, and today, they rush into the day without a plan for ensuring victory tomorrow. When I reflect on my own personal challenges and the obstacles that I overcame, I felt compelled to inspire others to do the same. While there are some aspects in life that are beyond your control, many are within your grasp. All that is required is the expense of a little effort to shape the outcome of our circumstance, and ultimately change the direction of your life. My intent is not to engage in an ethereal discussion that leads nowhere, but rather to engage in a discussion that awakens the realization of your purpose with passion and confidence. This book provides just that: a month-long guide that offers helpful insights that are designed to inspire life changing outcomes, and the discovery of your voice, purpose, and ultimately, your destiny.

It's November 6th, 2014, and I'm sitting at my desk preparing to start another day on my first prime contract. The cool fall Thursday morning starts with my daily devotional reading to help me set the tone for the day. I fire up my computer, review upcoming project milestones, and jump right into the activities planned for the day. As I rattle the keys of my keyboard which resemble the sounds of rapid-fire on military front lines, I hear a voice say: *I blessed you publicly, yet you would not share your testimony publicly.* Aghast, the rapid fire of my keyboard suddenly stops as I ponder the words of that voice. With an attitude of gratefulness, I recede into a contrite position, open a new document, and begin to type. As inspiration danced with reflection, I seize the moment to chronicle the journey that God brought me through. This is what followed—the Facebook post titled, "The Testimony I Never Shared."

Prologue:
The Testimony I Never Shared

IT IS 9 A.M. ON MARCH 14TH, 2014. My wife and I are at the settlement table selling a home that has been on the market for over six months. Denise and I are elated…FINALLY! Then my phone goes off and I step out of the room. On the other end is my vendor reporting to me that "your services are no longer needed." My joy immediately turns to tears…and more tears, as my wife of almost fifteen years and I sit in our car and weep profusely!

The story really starts in January 2014, when we both decided to pursue God on a forty-day fast. The book, *The Circle Maker*, was our daily devotional guide. It was a remarkable journey since we knew that the year of 2014 was going to be the year of transition! During this time we prayed for many things; however, I really wanted to experience growth in three main areas of business: (a) ChangeDynamix—our IT/Management Consulting practice, (b) joDah Ministries—our music philanthropy arm that helps Christian artists, and (c) ARK Recording Studio—our full-service recording facility.

In a very real way, God answered the first part of that prayer on that cloudy March morning, ironically, through an untimely lay-off that lasted not one month, not two, not three, but four and a half months! For the first time, I applied for unemployment and started a very lonesome journey into discovering a new path going forward. I remained numbed by the question that plagued my mind: How does someone with a PhD and other industry credentials end up in the unemployment line? I began 'hitting' Monster, Career Builder, and other such places, and received numerous interviews only to be told, "Sir, you are too good to be true…your credentials are outstanding BUT we can't afford you." Then, during the quietude of a devotion time in April, preparing for yet another State interview, God asked me the question: "How can you grow your own IT management consulting practice while working for SOMEONE else?" This was the missing piece of the puzzle that placed deep conviction upon my heart: **You can't really reach your full potential building someone else's dreams!**

Fast forward to July: the phone rings, and on the other end is the CEO of the very company that edged me out of the running for what was supposed to be a five-year contract. She said: "We would like to offer you a three month subcontract since our project manager is no longer available: the contract that we thought would last five years only turned out to be three months!" With no concern for the circumstances that led to this call, I was elated to have received it. This call led to my very first contract for my IT consulting practice, ending my drought of unemployment.

Now fast-forward to August 2014: I am sitting in my car waiting to pick up my sons from school when my phone rings. On the other end, the procurement officer from another State agency inquired, "Is this Dr. Josiah?" I quickly replied, "I am he!" What followed was a discussion about my availability for a project that I interviewed for BUT again, came in second to over 35 other companies. "We are considering you for a State award since the first vendor may no longer be eligible for the award." This meant that a contract 'fell through,' as they would say in the land of procurement. I was beyond ELATED since this would not only be my first prime contract, but the first multi-year State contract for my consulting practice—albeit seven months later. I should also add that I started my company (ChangeDynamix) seven years prior without turning a profit until 2014. I'll leave that there since over and over again I continue to be amazed at God's perfection in numbers!

Today, while I stay active in music production through ARK Recording Studio and joDah Ministries, my consulting practice is beginning to take shape. I remain humbled that God has entrusted these three special organizations to me and I am completely trusting Him for where He is about to take my family and me.

Much also can be said about joDah Ministries and ARK Recording Studio, but fearing that this turns into a book, I will stop here. However, I must hasten to add that neither I nor my family was in need during this four-and-a-half-month period of unemployment.

To my loving and devoted wife, Denise; to two

wonderful yet unsuspecting boys, Darryl and Derwen; and to a close knit family of friends in the DMV, I say thanks. Through the trial of 2014, I have become a stronger man, a wiser spiritual leader, a more devoted husband, and more importantly, the priest God would have me to be.

If you are going through the turmoil of change in your life, take it from me: God is a provider like no one else can be. He knows all, He sees all, and He cares. Trust Him with your worry, and watch Him turn your weeping into abundant joy!

———————

Within minutes after wondering whether or not I should have been this transparent, the first reply came: "Wow, I needed this today. Thank you for sharing this testimony."This was immediately followed by, "Truly needed this!" It seemed that I had struck a nerve, and before long, another reply kissed my timeline: "What a testimony! Nothing is too big for God to handle! And He's still writing your testimony! Thank you for sharing an inspiring way to start the day!" This was shortly followed by: "Thanks for your testimony! I sooo needed to hear this right now. God Bless." I began to realize that this experience was not just about me being vulnerable, but more so me being obedient to post a testimony that was now getting ready to bless so many others.

Shortly after, a close friend posted, "I'm wiping away the tears as I read this, Donnell. What a revelation of God's work in your life. He favors those who are obedient to the call, and praise God you answered that call. You & Denise are truly a testament of God's wonderful love for us. I know this is just a taste of what He has in store for your family. Love you!" Before long, another reply trickled in: "To God be all the Glory!!! Thank you for sharing...someone will overcome because of this testimony." The title of this book—*Overcomers*—came from this reply. Tears began to fill my eyes as I saw first-hand the transformative power of what a testimony can do.

Being overwhelmed, I got up from my computer to wash my blood-shot eyes. Upon returning to my desk, I was greeted with more touching responses from family, friends, and acquaintances. Couples who were in the midst of difficult circumstances, along with individuals who recently lost their jobs, responded with sincerity. One came from a couple with whom I am well acquainted: "Like everyone else who has commented, I needed to hear this today!! Thank you for your transparency. I pray God will continue to lead & use you as you continue to seek Him first!" This was followed by, "Thank you so much for sharing this, Donnell S. Josiah! I've been in a season of transition and re-scoping lately, and while it's not over yet, I take your experience as evidence that God is REALLY working behind the scenes even when we can't see movement." I was convinced that I made the right decision, and that it was the right season and right time to share my testimony with the world.

What also became clear to me was that many individuals also shared similar life challenges, choosing to quietly endure their emotional and mental pain alone. This was evident by the following message: "Donnell S. Josiah, praise God for His unconditional love. Your testimony is truly a blessing to me. This morning I was frustrated about something that seems to be taking forever, but my husband told me to calm down. It was in that moment that I realized we [were] going through what God [needed for us to go through so that we can] become stronger. You are right about 2014 being a year of transition. We have been hit with many challenges that made us try God. It has made us wiser, stronger, and more dedicated to Him and each other. Keep testifying because God gives us the trial so we can have a testimony. God bless you and the family." Equally reflective was another reply that said: "Thank you so much for sharing your testimony!!! Sometimes we live our lives and have no idea what our brothers and sisters are going through. I needed this today, as I am going through my longest period of unemployment as a new single mom. But God is literally providing for me day by day. For it is in the darkness that God performs a transformation that could not otherwise be made. I praise God for the work He is doing in us. My LOVE and Prayers to your family!!!"

Over the next several hours, the post received more thoughtful responses and before long over one hundred responses littered my time-line. Responses started coming in from around the world, some of which were very touching. One came from someone who knew me as a child as he eloquently stated: "To God be all the glory, my brother. I share a similar experience. My unemployment was 18 months, but like David, God never saw me forsaken or begging bread. He has opened so many doors for me; to God be the glory." The part that was immensely touching was: "Not trying to stir up any memories, but Mom should be here to hear or read this testimony. Much appreciative of this testimony, Donnell. It just reassures me that the God we serve is always there to see us through ANY situation. Keep pressing on and let God lead. Sis. P (Pearline) would surely be proud of her true go-getter. God bless my friend."

The reason this last post was so touching is because I still struggle with coping with my Mom's passing, although it's been over three years. I have always been very close to my family, but my Mom and I shared a very special bond. So to have individuals, who not only knew me from my roots in Antigua, but who also knew my Mom dearly, post such a heart-moving response, was nothing short of a tear-jerker! However, the post that really connected to my heart was that of a long-lost brother, who while not sharing the same birth mother, was just as close to me as my lone biological brother. You see, for several years our friendship grew estranged and we lost contact; however, after reading my post he posted this very touching response: "My Little Brother Donnell. I publicly apologize for absenting myself from you, my niece, and nephews. I'm sorry for not being there to know and help comfort you through your crucible, having been there on more than one instance. I am now and will continue to check on you to stand by and with you through thick and thin. Please forgive me. My mind races back to the counsel I gave you so many years ago during your teenage years and at the infancy of your expressed dreams while you yet resided in Antigua and Barbuda, the land of our birth! I repeated the same advice to you at your wedding to your lovely and Godly wife, Denise. Today, I wish to assure you of the fulfillment of God's unfailing promise to you then, and its magnanimous establishment now. Review, if you will, the text I've repeatedly shared with you over the years-Proverbs 22:29. May I suggest, once again, that you take some focused time and become intimately acquainted with its inherent spiritual comfort? I genuinely love you! Your big brother."

Clearly, my post connected with many people on a number of levels. I began getting requests from people wanting to read more of my journey—the journey of the unsuspecting rise of a lanky computer technician and musician who started from very humble beginnings. The journey of a teen labeled as an "academic failure," but who later ascended into positions of leadership as a result of his work ethic, persistence, and commitment to excellence. As I looked back over this journey, I must concede that it was quite a journey indeed. Now as an adult, I see the alignment of my struggle with God's destiny over my life. My Facebook post was just the beginning of my awakening to the realization that I have many more people to inspire, many more goals to reach, and many more lives to change.

Whatever your situation, know that *Overcomers* was written just for you. *Overcomers* was written for those feeling 'down and out' and possibly experiencing disappointment in many areas of their lives. On the other hand, *Overcomers* will also challenge the ambitious and goal-oriented person who may have lost their passion but is earnestly seeking a way back to achieve their life's purpose. *Overcomers* will restore voice to those who have gone silent as a result of defeat. *Overcomers* will give strength to those seeking to move past yesterday's obstacles, breathing new life into dreams that went lifeless for way too long.

So as you take this journey with me for the next thirty-one days, consider that this book was written by someone no different from you. Keep in mind that this book was written by a lanky guy from a rural Caribbean village who was labeled as a 'nobody' before God's favor transformed him into becoming a 'somebody.' Yes, I have overcome much in my lifetime, but know that if I can do it, so can you! The question is: are you ready to get inspired to find your purpose, passion, and voice as you pursue your dreams? Get ready, because the change you have been waiting for is closer than you think. Today is your day. It's your time, it's your turn, and it's your year to become an overcomer. Are you ready? Let's go!

1.

My Early Days

Chapter Goal: *Think about your journey, your joys and your struggles. Now think about your dreams. Decide to pursue them today!*

IT'S 9:00 A.M. AND THE FIRST school bell rings. Everyone freezes until the second bell rings before sprinting towards their designated classroom doors. Located in the southern-most part of the twin-island nation of Antigua and Barbuda is Old Road Primary School, the school that introduced me to formal education. In this rural school, young minds were developed on the premise that all students could become anything they set their minds to. Each day we gathered for prayer; each day we listened to principal's stern voice demanding nothing less than our best. These are not only the memories I have of my primary school, but these are the memories that would serve as the catalyst for my academic pursuits, way into my adult years.

Fast-forward to my high school years: I was tall, lanky, and promised a bright future subject to good grades. I had an insatiable appetite for learning and a love for Physics, Chemistry, and a host of other subject areas. Each day I looked at the school motto, "Success through Sustained Effort," that was painted in a semi-circular arch on the back wall of the school's auditorium. This motto inspired me as I prepared to undergo a rigorous battery of tests, administered by the Caribbean Examination Council (CXC).

I was the youngest person in my class and the time had come to register for the numbing CXC exams that would test all that I learned in my five years of high school. The day of registration, being confident in my own abilities, I registered for testing in nine subject areas. That morning, on my way to class, the principal called me into her office. Thinking that it was out of admiration for my prior academic successes, I was stunned when she informed me that she was not going to authorize me taking such a heavy academic load due to my age. I sat there befuddled as she attempted to convince me of her decision that would only allow me to sit five subjects—almost half of what I was capable. I was disappointed and distraught, but decided to fight the decision with the School Board of Education. Unfortunately, after weeks of pleading my case, the Board of Education thought it best not to overrule the decision of the principal. Given my love for physical and natural science, I registered to sit exams in Physics, Chemistry, Mathematics, English, and Geography. Conflicted by the motto that inspired me to dream big dreams and to become great at whatever was possible, I felt defeated. I, however, remained committed to putting my 'best foot forward' and to excel in the five subject areas that I was allowed to take. The next few months presented formidable challenges because of the sudden and unforeseen lack of teaching resources for the subjects I had registered to take. My chances of success became even more dismal, compounded by the fact that I now had to travel to neighboring schools to receive supplemental aid. Through it all, my mother would encourage me through a little poem that she engraved in our minds:

The go-getter goes till he gets what he goes for.
The go-getter works till he reaps what he sows for.
He fixes a goal and resolves when he sets it.
The way to the prize is to go till he gets it.

Feeling defeated, disappointed, and at times very discouraged, the words that rang over and over in my head were, "the way to the prize is to go till he gets it."

"The go-getter goes till he gets what he goes for. The go-getter works till he reaps what he sows for. He fixes a goal and resolves when he sets it. The way to the prize is to go till he gets it."
Susan M. Willoughby

One of the things I had to learn was that life's lesson on fairness was not going to be taught in the dusty classrooms of Jennings Secondary High School. I had to dig deep and believe in myself even when my principal didn't. I had to commit myself to overcoming the emotional and academic struggles that confronted me, while I worked at a deficit to compete with my fellow classmates. I had to accept and believe that while some of my teachers retired, resigned, or simply abandoned my prospect of learning, that one day I would be an overcomer—someone who my parents would be proud of. While some may have given up and become a casualty of the system, these obstacles began teaching me what it meant to be an overcomer, preparing me for the next phase that was about to come.

Reflection: *The journey to your destiny is conceived through your dreams, awoken through conviction, pursued through pain, and achieved through passion.*

2.

Results that Matter

Chapter Goal: *Begin believing in yourself and your God-given ability to achieve your goals, regardless of your past!*

THE SUMMER VACATION DRAWS TO a close and the day arrives for me to collect my examination results. Everyone is on edge. The principal is about to learn how her students fared in relation to other schools, the outcome being a reflection of her leadership. The teachers are also on pins and needles since their students' academic performance would also be a reflection of their tutelage. But these test results mattered to no one more than me, since this would be the defining moment that determined my college-worthiness. The trajectory of my academic life would be determined by the number of CXC subjects I was able to pass. Staring me dead in the face was the bleak reminder that I started my academic race at a significant disadvantage—a disadvantage set in motion the moment when I was disallowed to take my desired subjects, and a disadvantage that would plague me for the rest of my foreseeable future forcing me to play 'catch-up' to my fellow classmates.

It's my turn to learn my fate. I hear "Donnell Josiah, this way" as I get called into the office to collect my results. Quietly trembling, I opened my envelope and what I saw crushed me. My performance was average at best, especially when compared to other students who excelled in their subject areas. In the months that followed, I questioned, why? What happened? Am I not smart enough? Struggling to determine how I would overcome my own academic underachievement, I heard God's voice quietly reminding me, "No, my son, you were not prepared enough."

This perspective was the redeeming hope that I needed to not slide into teenage depression. While my classmates and family members boasted of their academic successes and entrance into college, I struggled feeling ill-equipped to make the grade. Some looked upon my average academic performance with disdain, almost rendering my future pursuits as hopeless. However, with two loving parents at my side, and a brother and sister who encouraged me to keep fighting, I pushed forward. Now labeled an academic failure in the eyes of some, I was even more determined to prove to myself that I could be anything I put my mind to despite the insurmountable odds that now confronted me. Given my love for science and an incredible knack for electronics, I

Do it right the first time, and every time!

was drawn to pursuing further study. But how? Where do I go with sub-par academic performance? Well, you enter the workforce.

It's a typical Tuesday afternoon, and we are making our usual run to the city. My dad pulls into the parking area for a well-known business—E. Alex Benjamin Limited. Seeking an entry-level position for me, Dad proceeded to describe my abilities, interests, and desires to the managing director. The conversation with Mr. 'Paddy' Benjamin continued for quite some time as it seemed certain that I would land my first job right out of high school. The conversation took a turn when out of Dad's gratitude for considering me for the position, I heard him say, "You don't even have to pay him anything!" I violently screamed to myself, "Are you out of your mind?" What I later realized was the wisdom of Dad's approach, since he knew that I would be an incredible asset to whomever would choose to hire me. Mr. Benjamin didn't have to agree to bring me under his wings, but he did. I learned some of life's most important lessons from him—lessons that further prepared me to become an overcomer. I could still hear him say, "Sport, do it right first time, and every time!" This life lesson, coupled with the great people with whom I worked, cemented my interest in engineering. Through Dad's wisdom, Mr. Benjamin's kindness, and God's providence, this first job forever reshaped my self-confidence and my self-esteem, and solidified a new interest in becoming an engineer. Overcomers may not always see the end from the beginning, but overcomers take advantage of opportunities that allow them to walk into their destiny. Overcomers believe in themselves and that God will orchestrate transitions that last a lifetime.

Reflection: *Failure and defeat may sometime assail you, but their occurrence must not be permanent.*

3.
Transition of a Lifetime

Chapter Goal: *Acquire new knowledge, develop new skills, and invest in building new relationships today.*

IT'S MONDAY MORNING AND I show up for my first day of work. I immediately noticed the jovial white-bearded gentleman who would later be introduced as my supervisor. With a broad smile on his face, Mr. Conrad 'Connie' Doram asked, "So what's your name?" I responded somewhat cautiously, "My name is Donnell Josiah, but most folks call me Sport." Connie showed me around the office that morning, introducing me as the new addition to his staff. That moment signaled the beginning of a long friendship with some of the best electronic technicians in the country! For the next eight years this experienced group of technicians poured into my mental sponge their wisdom amassed over years of working in the field. One of these individuals was a computer technician who introduced me to Cleveland Institute of Electronics, redeeming my quest for academic advancement. What Mr. Casey didn't know was that he was an answer to prayer. Days later, the overcomer in me leaped with joy after the information packet arrived in the mail, providing information about the school's distance learning programs.

After a few days of reviewing the information packet, and seriously considering the possibility of continuing education, I was convinced that the Associates Degree program in Electronics Engineering would become my next academic frontier. Over the next few weeks, I applied for enrollment and was accepted to start the program. The next four years would prove daunting, often leaving me questioning if I made the right decision. I should have noticed the school's motto: "A school of thousands, a class of one," but apparently, I missed this important detail. You see, most engineering programs are delivered through the traditional classroom environment. Engineering programs are also often very rigorous, so to undertake a program of study through distance learning was borderline crazy! Over the next four years I would often feel completely overwhelmed, being unable to grasp the heavy mathematical courses such as Calculus, Furrier Analysis, and Transient Analysis. However, remembering Mom's counsel, I would wipe away my tears, pick up the books yet again, and continue pressing forward believing that I would one day overcome this academic challenge. Four years later, I did, graduating with an Associate's degree in Electronic Engineering. This was the first and most important step towards rejecting the notions of those who had long held opinions about my prior academic underachievement. It was also, and more importantly, my first chance at entering college, allowing me to pursue my destiny.

> **Education does not promise you anything, but education prepares you for everything!**

One day as I returned to the office, I received a service call from one of the area banks. A critical computer system would not boot threatening end of month processing. I quickly collected my tools and rushed to the site and within the hour I was able to carry out an operation averting service interruption. The branch manager and I sat down in conversation in which he asked me about my goals and academic interests. As I described my interest in higher education, he interrupted me: "I need you to call the Director for the Organization of American States— Dr. Kenneth Jordan— right away." He provided me his number and as soon as I returned to my desk I quickly reached out to Dr. Jordan. Several conversations later, I competed and won a fully funded international fellowship that offered me a chance of a lifetime. While education does not promise you anything, education prepares you for everything!

As you will later discover in this book, this fellowship enabled me to migrate to the United States to fulfill my dreams of becoming an engineer. Now, as I look back over my life with immense gratitude, I am humbled and blessed to have overcome many obstacles. I still reflect on the school mottoes from my childhood that inspired me through the years. Indeed, overcomers "Endeavor to Learn and Go Forth to Serve" recognizing that "Success" only comes "Through Sustained Effort." Overcomers embrace challenges versus running from them. Like me, overcomers may be rendered academic failures, but I have learned that overcomers work hard, they value education, they pursue their purpose, and they later achieve their destiny.

Reflection: *Meaningful life transitions are often determined by your readiness to leverage knowledge, skills, and relationships.*

4.

Purpose

Chapter Goal: *Invest one hour today pursuing that 'one thing' that gives you fulfillment and satisfaction.*

HAVE YOU EVER ASKED YOURSELF the following questions: Why am I here? What is my purpose? Where am I going? These are not only familiar questions college grads ask, but these are often questions that remain unanswered for some even through their adult years. Unfortunately, for a number of reasons, many individuals find themselves wandering through life unable to define their life's purpose, and sadly, never reaching their full potential.

Purpose is the conviction that results when passion and talent converge. Purpose is not to be confused with talent. While talent may equip you with the skills that are necessary to perform a particular task, if the task does not result in a conviction that aligns with your passion and talent, then the task itself may be a distraction from you achieving your true purpose. For example, many individuals place objects on pianos as if they were expensive bookshelves. While the piano can withstand the weight of many books, its primary function is not to store books! Rather, when placed under the touch of a master pianist, the piano erupts into music, thereby accomplishing its intended purpose.

In his book, *The Purpose Driven Life*, Rick Warren suggests that true meaning and significance in life often come from understanding and fulfilling God's purpose for your life. Like the piano, we sometimes find ourselves functioning in roles that we either were forced into, or roles that we assumed simply to appease someone else's expectations. These are examples of misdirected energy that often do not aid in discovering your true purpose. However, when conviction collides with your talent and passion, the result often is the realization of your highest calling— your purpose.

In 1998, when I migrated to the United States to pursue higher education, I had an intriguing conversation with a young lady who was a gifted singer and who was also passionate about counseling children. We conversed for hours about the many beautiful ways in which her talent of music converged with her passion for school counseling. Sixteen years later, she is still an awesome singer, school counselor, and now the mother of my children.

Overcomers pursue their passion in life because it ultimately leads them to their purpose. Overcomers are not distracted with unnecessary activities that simply consume their time; rather, overcomers engage in activities that fuel their passion, develop their talents, and reward their efforts. It's time to live your dreams, but you must start with **When conviction collides with your talent and passion, the result often is the realization of your highest calling—your purpose!** understanding your purpose. Don't squander your life chasing someone else's dream. Stop, think, and dig deep inside, listen to your inner voice, and sure enough you will soon find the point where your inner passion collides with the talent that God placed within you.

Reflection: *Fulfillment in life occurs when your vocation aligns with your passion and purpose.*

5.

The Inner Voice

Chapter Goal: *Rewrite each label used to describe your past with another that defines your future.*

YOU'VE HEARD IT, AND PROBABLY more times than you care to admit: the taunts that wound your self-worth, the attacks that immobilize your sense of purpose, the parental rage that numbs the voice of a child who aspires to become somebody great. Deafening are the words: "You're a nobody"; "You're not smart enough"; "You're never going to amount to anything." These are words that incinerate your purpose and silence your inner voice. These verbal daggers often make deep puncture wounds—wounds inflicted by individuals who lack the understanding of human dignity, and who have little value, appreciation, and knowledge of human potential. But deep inside, your inner voice retorts, "It's a lie," setting in motion a life destined to beat the odds.

Born into a middle class family was a young man who was thought to be an underachiever. He had loving parents who gave him all they had, but despite their giving of unwavering love, they could not afford him the privilege of attending university. In his early years he was curious, and was comfortable being alone, preferring to spend time exploring his surroundings versus tumbling with the boys in the village. He was labeled shy and was uncomfortable speaking in public. In class he would often become bored by the inflexible teaching styles that did not offer him much challenge. His mother, being the strong-willed woman that she was, instilled in him the love for music. As if to inspire his quest for deeper learning, she would ignite his curiosity for what would later become his love of science. Each day as he sat amongst his fellow classmates, his teachers were unaware that the lad who sat in front of their instruction was Albert Einstein—the man who one day would later be regarded as the greatest scientist of the 20th century, and whose work will go on to change the world forever. In spite of the labels that he had to overcome as a youngster, some partly for questioning the accepted wisdom of the day, Einstein stayed true to himself, believing in himself, and through his inquiring mind, challenged what seemed to many as the immutable boundaries of knowledge.

Einstein's story is not unique. Unfortunately, many students like myself became victims of academic systems that subjected them to stereotypes. Saddled with labels that often ill-define their true potential, students wrestle with identities that are imposed upon them—identities that sometimes last a lifetime. Overcomers are not immune; rather, overcomers listen to their inner voice that compels them to triumph over their circumstances. While you may not be considered as gifted as Albert Einstein, deep within you is a resource

> **It's not too late to live the life that is ordered by your purpose!**

of immense potential that is waiting to come to the surface. Deep within you is an inner voice that refuses to succumb to the labels and stereotypes that may have been imposed upon you. This is your chance to believe again. This is your chance to pursue again the dreams that you once held as your resolve. It's not too late—it's never too late to live the life that is ordered by your purpose.

Like Einstein, overcomers may appear different, but it's their difference that positions them for greatness. Embrace this difference and speak life over yourself, because, on their way to greatness, overcomers withstand the jabs of their doubters by listening to their inner voice that says, "I am somebody," "I am smart enough," "I will amount to anything I put my mind to" because "Greatness resides within me!" Overcomers reject having someone rewrite their future simply because they are ill-equipped to see it. Overcomers believe in themselves, speak positive words, and think positive thoughts as they climb the ladder of success. Overcomers exercise willpower, because it is the key that unlocks their purpose, and the catalyst that activates their destiny. Like overcomers, you too, can become anything you set your mind to. Now is your moment to silence the naysayers and those who may have rendered you useless. Regain the position that God destined just for you. Obey His words, trust His heart, seek His guidance, and listen to your inner voice.

Reflection: *Your inner voice is best heard when life's competing noises are silenced by your purpose.*

6.

Willpower, Your Key to Success

Chapter Goal: *Commit to pursuing three goals today. Challenge yourself to complete each goal before the end of the day.*

EXHAUSTED AFTER WHAT SEEMED TO be a marathon following our recent move, I sat back with my sons to survey the progress. What followed was their introduction to one of life's most important lessons—the lesson about willpower. Sitting around the empty boxes that littered the floor, I coined a phrase that will probably stick with them for the rest of their lives: **When something is needed to be done, stick with it until it gets done!** Willpower, the ability to resist short-term pains for long-term gains, is arguably one of the most important determinants for success. Without willpower, goals often go unachieved, success unattained, and the hope of achieving one's purpose in life often goes unfulfilled. While some place willpower within the confines of self-control, and others describe it as the ability to prevail over unwanted thoughts, feelings, or impulses, how is willpower developed, and why is it the key to success and long-term happiness? Let's take a closer look.

Willpower is a depletable psychological resource that influences personal decision making. Willpower creates the drive to pursue personal goals, and the lack of it often results in behaviors that ultimately lead to disappointment. Willpower wrestles with the mind to control actions of the body. Willpower focuses action towards the attainment of meaningful goals. Willpower is the key differentiator between individuals who achieve great success in life versus those who simply endure it. Consider for a moment the differences between individuals who are successful IN life versus those who are successful AT life. The main difference is the power of the will to inspire and compel action. Willpower compels you to get

Involved in the pursuit of your own goals, equipping you to become successful IN life versus AT life. In contrast, the absence of willpower often results in aimless wandering through life; hence the connotation, successful AT life. When willpower is depleted, life simply happens without the intentional effort to pursue meaningful goals. That's why for the overcomer, willpower compels action forcing them to adopt an attitude of perseverance in the midst of insurmountable challenges. Like a muscle, willpower must be built. It must be stretched in order to grow. It blossoms through self-denial and flourishes through the attainment of goals that are set. Willpower is ignited when the pain of maintaining the status quo is outweighed by the need for making a life change. For example, the pain in pursuing an academic degree is outweighed by the derived benefits received after its completion.

> **When something is needed to be done, stick with it until it gets done!**

But how do overcomers learn to pursue long-term happiness in place of enjoying the ease of short-term gratification? The first step is determining the real motivation for change, answering the fundamental question: why is change needed in the first place? What is at risk if I choose not to change? What are the health consequences? How will my career, my family, or my relationships be impacted if I do not take the steps today to secure a more promising future? Answers to these questions provide motivational opportunities to exercise one's willpower. The second step requires setting bite-sized goals that are attainable each day—goals that are aligned with one's purpose, passion, and vision. Now that motivation has been established, and a plan has been devised to meet these daily goals, the third step requires measuring your progress on a daily basis to track the degree to which you are meeting your goals. Each time you engage in purposeful activity, you strengthen your will, taking small steps towards the attainment of your goals. The contrary is true: each time you give in to inactivity and procrastination, you weaken the muscle of your will, rendering it useless through atrophy.

Overcomers understand the immense value of willpower, since it shapes their work-ethic and fosters an attitude that pushes them beyond the brink of comfort and into the promise of their life's purpose. Developing the will really starts in your mind; it starts with developing positive attitudes because attitudes matter. So, pursue your goals with relentless conviction and take the steps necessary towards fulfilling a purpose driven life. Remember, the path to your prize is through perseverance. Push through the limits and pursue your dreams.

Reflection: *Willpower is like a muscle; it must be stretched in order to grow.*

7.

Attitude Matters

Chapter Goal: *For each emotion, thought, and action, ask yourself the question: will my attitude help or hinder my chances of reaching my goal?*

THE ALARM CLOCK RINGS, YOUR sleep is suddenly disturbed, and a new day filled with opportunity now waits. Within the deep recesses of your mind two decisions begin to form: do I roll out of bed and get ready for a new day, or do I steal an extra hour or two under the warm covers? There are times when life's urgencies demand that you jump out of bed and run into action, and there are other times when physical exhaustion demands that you rest, even for a little while longer. Taken in isolation, either of these options is not wrong; however, your general predisposition to either of these outcomes reveals very interesting insights—insights that often determine the outcome of your day. While the overcomer is not immuned from either of these outcomes, they understand the importance of shielding themselves from developing attitudes that limit, versus cultivating attitudes that build up. Overcomers recognize that attitudes shape decisions, and decisions ultimately result in actions—actions that either hinder or aid the attainment of your personal goals.

It has often been said that a person's attitude determines their altitude. Attitude is the collection of one's mental, emotional, and behavioral predisposition to personal and/or societal factors. Attitudes represent complex constructs of one's mind and have been described as having three important components: (a) an affective component that reveals a person's feelings and emotions, (b) a behavioral component that triggers one's response to their feelings and emotions, and (c) a cognitive component that rationalizes actual facts against individually constructed beliefs. For example, your fear of pursuing higher education may cause you to immerse yourself in daily activities that consume all your time and resources. These activities are then rationalized as being too essential to interrupt the flow of life for the sake of continuing education. The result? Years fly past and your goals go unfulfilled. Each time the decision is made to excuse action for inaction, the dangerous cycle takes deeper root making the attainment of your goals so much more difficult to reach. Ultimately, the interplay of mental, emotional, and behavioral constructs shape your priorities, that's why it's essential to have a positive attitude, and to define small measurable goals that channel your focus on pursuing your life's purpose that in the end brings you one step closer to reaching your destiny.

Attitudes inform your thoughts, your thoughts produce action, and your action—or lack thereof—dictates who you become.

A positive attitude shapes your entire outlook and serves as the catalyst for your own success. Positive attitudes instill confidence, motivate action, and inspire hope. Despite life's conflicting web of circumstances, a positive attitude focuses one's response on productive outcomes rather than negative consequences. This is especially true for the overcomer. Overcomers don't have fewer problems; they simply adjust their attitude and choose to respond differently to them. Overcomers identify the hidden fears and biases that often influence their initial response—the response that excuses versus the response that produces. Overcomers cultivate positive attitudes because attitudes inform your thoughts, your thoughts produce action, and your action—or lack thereof—dictates who you become.

In a world riddled with social, emotional, and economic tensions it's easy to see how twisted ideologies, ill-constructed belief systems, and rogue value systems can shape a person's outlook on life. However, if we take the time to cultivate positive attitudes, we may very well open up ourselves to experiencing the true essence of positive living. Borrowing from the words of Mahatma Gandhi: "Your attitude shapes your beliefs; Your beliefs become your thoughts; Your thoughts become your words; Your words become your actions; Your actions become your habits; Your habits become your values; Your values become your destiny." Overcomers shape their destiny by cultivating positive attitudes—attitudes that enable them to change the world around them.

Reflection: *Attitude shapes behaviors and behaviors inform action. Cultivate positive attitudes and reap the harvest of positive living.*

8.

Passion

Chapter Goal: *Direct your attention and energy toward those things that bring you one step closer to reaching your destiny.*

IT'S DECEMBER 31ST AND THE CLOCK begins its countdown. Months of preparation, including planning daily meetings, enterprise system expansions, mainframe upgrades, and a host of other application changes must now be put to the real test. I initiate the roll call and my technical teams located all across the country are accounted for. Everyone is ready! On the conference bridge are senior US Department of Education representatives and a team of engineers ready to respond to any eventuality. Within minutes, the new FAFSA application is in production and students from around the country begin submitting their applications for federal student aid. Each year, the US Department of Education goes through this exhaustive process to ensure that they are prepared to accept applications for over 16 million students annually. Despite the trends that show an increase in financial aid applications for first-time, full-time undergraduate students at 4-year degree-granting institutions, many students make a pivotal mistake of pursuing higher education without a clear sense of their purpose, and many lack the passion to pursue it. Inevitably, time is wasted and much hard-earned money is squandered pursuing academic programs for which they have no interest. Why bother? Why sit through hours of lectures and days of assignments only to later discover something more exciting, rewarding, and more meaningful? Where is the passion—the depth of conviction for pursuing your life's purpose?

Passion is the strong emotional drive that compels action. Passion beats in time with the heart, directing focus to that which provides deeper meaning. Passion is the 'thing' you enjoy doing, and would enjoy doing even if you were not adequately compensated. Passion is the catalyst that arouses action in pursuit of your purpose.

Denzel Washington, in an inspirational speech to young aspiring actors, outlined his recipe for success: "True desire in the heart for anything good is God's proof to you sent beforehand to indicate that it's yours already." Passion, the seat of your obsession, the thing that produces the most meaning, and thus the thing that you would 'love to live to do,' is God's gift, assurance, and cosigned proof of His intention for your life. Passion requires you to acknowledge it. Diligence requires you to chase it. Purpose demands that you have it. Favor compels that you claim it, and God's provision assures that you receive it!

Passion without direction equals misdirection, and passion without consistency results in misapplied energy!

Overcomers pursue their passion with hopes of achieving the purpose for their life. Purpose, birthed in their dreams, is activated through persistence and diligence. Diligence enables them to chase their goals, since according to Washington, "dreams without goals remain dreams—just dreams." While many people seem to wander through life without passion and an understanding of their life's purpose, overcomers are different. They chart a course that unites their purpose with their passion recognizing that unfulfilled dreams will inevitably fuel disappointment.

Washington ends his speech with a foreboding reminder that "goals, on the road to achievement, cannot be achieved without discipline and consistency." Passion without direction is nothing more than misdirection, and passion without consistency results in misapplied energy. Overcomers pursue their dreams with diligence and consistency resisting the urge to trade long-term happiness for the security of another paycheck. Overcomers chase happiness, seek fulfillment, and make it their life's purpose to find their deeper meaning to life. Overcomers push past their fears, confronting the unknown in pursuit of the known. Overcomers follow their dreams with passion, discipline, and consistency and help others within their influence to do the same.

Reflection: *Passion is the catalyst that arouses action in pursuit of that 'one thing' that produces the most meaning for you.*

9.

Discipline

Chapter Goal: *Define boundaries that guide you towards accomplishing your goals.*

WHEN DENZEL WASHINGTON, IN HIS inspirational speech to young aspiring actors, outlined his recipe for success he emphasized the importance of two words: (a) discipline, and (b) consistency. He said "goals, on the road to achievement, cannot be achieved without discipline and consistency." Dreams will remain dreams, art will remain unpainted, relationships will remain untapped, music will remain without melody, and life will remain fruitless unless consistent effort is applied in its daily pursuit. In the previous chapter I described the importance of being passionate about pursuing and achieving your dreams. Passion is the emotional drive that compels action and directs focus to that which provides deeper meaning. It's the 'thing' you enjoy doing, and would enjoy doing even if you were not adequately compensated. However, overcomers need more than passion in order to achieve success; they need to exercise discipline in all areas of their life.

Discipline is the exercise of deliberate thought and action that governs behavior. Discipline causes one to define boundaries through self-imposed rules in order to make positive change. Discipline provides the thrust in the engine of passion that propels you towards your goals. Discipline regulates desire and focuses attention on meeting needs versus wants. Discipline seeks to delay gratification of tomorrow's benefits by focusing on the work that is required today.

Recently, I was conflicted when faced with making a pretty large electronic purchase. The purchase would have provided me significant benefits, improved workflow, and greater efficiency. I secured numerous quotes, checked out all needed components, but was not fully 'sold' on making the purchase. After a few days of mulling it over in my mind, I decided that while the new Apple Mac Pro computer was justifiably an important purchase for my operation, it was not urgent, nor was it expedient at the time. Self-discipline enabled me to suspend my personal desires, self interest, and convenience in consideration of more urgent needs. While I did later commit to the purchase, my delay allowed me to exercise self-discipline, and allowed me to think logically, practically, economically, and responsibly. But discipline is not only required for sound financial reasoning; it is also required for all matters of governance and stewardship. How many times did you relish the joys of immediate pleasure in the short-term, but in the end sacrifice long-term happiness? Where would your career, your life, your

> **Discipline provides the thrust in the engine of passion that propels you towards your goals!**

relationships be if you only decided to spend a fraction of your day focusing on pursuing and accomplishing meaningful outcomes for you and your family?

Discipline requires making this change: a change to commit time and resources on the things that truly matter. Discipline requires setting and following through with your commitments, both personal and professional. Discipline requires the exercise of self-control to guard the avenues of the mind, the soul, and the heart, restricting use of any object that can inflict injury—both physical and emotional. Discipline requires following healthy life choices that would promote healthy living and longer life. Discipline resists the urge to procrastinate on the little before your life is compromised by the much. Discipline causes you to create positive, healthy, and responsible habits that not only promote efficiency, but sets the standard for modeling positive behaviors to your peers, colleagues, and children. Overcomers exercise discipline in setting, measuring, and completing meaningful activities each day; activities that lead them one step closer towards the attainment of longer-term goals. Overcomers exercise discipline by prioritizing the use of their resources in pursuit of goals that really matter in the long-term. Simply put, overcomers strive to achieve discipline in all areas of their life. They spend time cultivating healthy habits that promote wholeness, wellness, and oneness with their God. Overcomers invest time doing that which is important not only for themselves, but also for the good of others and the communities they serve.

Reflection: *No one can achieve your goals for you. Take some time today to pursue the dreams that will bring you happiness tomorrow.*

10.

Consistency

Chapter Goal: *Break long-term goals into smaller segments of short-term goals, building momentum as you accomplish them each day.*

FOR MOST, THE HOLIDAYS ARE filled with fun, shopping, and a lot of food. Starting with the Thanksgiving splurge and continuing into the festive Yuletide season, the unmistakable increase for some people appears with gut-busting certainty. The promise of post-holiday fitness ensnares some to savor yet another delightful bite before realizing that they have long fallen off their proverbial wagons. Like clockwork, the start of the year rolls around and they commit to joining their local gym as memberships skyrocket at predictably alarming rates. By the second week in February, 80% of these well-meaning individuals quit, and the cycle begins all over again. Noble intentions are overrun by excuses, and the seed of hope never seems to blossom into fruits of meaningful change. Why? Is it because one's goals have shifted due to more attractive options? Or is it because one important ingredient is lacking—the ingredient of consistency?

Consistency is the measure of stability, stick-to-itiveness, and patience that is required to acquire a new skill. It is an essential enabler for personal success, and it is vital for all areas of life that require high degrees of performance. Consistency provides a predictable framework for producing reliable outcomes with minimal uncertainty and anxiety. It is less focused on quick fixes and governed more by one's pursuit of meaningful results that lead to long-term sustainable happiness. Consistency is not only essential in personal development, but is equally important in business. In business, even the most noble of plans fail because of a lack of consistency. Consistency requires commitment in the 'head' before results can be delivered in the 'hand'. This is because consistent actions can be measured, and measurement of these actions instills trust and accountability.

Let's be clear, building consistency requires a lot of effort considering that even the best of us fall victim to old habits. Old habits die hard and new ones take time to grow. That's why in their quest for consistency overcomers sequence their daily goals into easily attainable milestones and progressively move towards tackling more difficult ones. The accomplishment of short-term goals enables them to build momentum, accelerating them towards the attainment of longer-term goals. In the process, overcomers develop consistent habits, and what seemed to have been an elusive dream suddenly comes within reach. While dreams without goals remain dreams, success is not achieved simply by dreaming—everyone dreams. Success is not achieved purely by defining the goals—everyone sets them. Success is not a personal right of inheritance—if so we'll all be rich. Rather, success is the milepost at which discipline and consistency meet on the long road of purpose.

> **Success is the milepost at which discipline and consistency meet on the long road of purpose.**

When I think about consistency, I think about my now deceased Mom—Pearline Josiah. Why? Because her message of persistence and consistency parallels with the process by which pearls are made. Pearls are the only gemstone that is produced by a living organism. At the core of a pearl is a small irritant that enters the clasp of the oyster's shell. In order to lessen the irritation, the oyster covers the irritant with layers of a secreted substance called nacre. The oyster applies layer upon layer to the irritant, and over a period of time, the entombed irritant emerges as a hard, beautiful, and iridescent gemstone. Like my maternal 'Pearl' gemstone, overcomers persist through consistency, entombing the irritants of life with perseverance, diligence, and consistency. Before long the pearls of wisdom, achievement, and success emerge with iridescent luster. Consistency never breaks you; but the lack of it may very well kill you. Consistency always makes the difference for the overcomer because it separates success from failure.

Reflection: *Consistency is the glue that sticks conviction with passion, plans with goals, and purpose with destiny.*

11.

Success through Failure

Chapter Goal: *Redirect the negative energy that failure creates into positive, life-changing, and teachable opportunities.*

HE IS AT AN IMPORTANT transition in life and ready to explore his surroundings. His muscles are weak, but his resolve is strong. With a broad smile on his face and a twinkle in his eyes, he shouts "Dad-da." He puts one step forward as a long drool escapes his open mouth. Cheering him on are Mom and Dad: "Come on, buddy, you can do it!" Before long, Darryl falls to the carpet with a strong resolve to try again. This essential process of learning to walk represents a critical period in the life of the toddler. Like Darryl, toddlers quickly rebound from their repeated falls, grabbing tightly to the hand that teaches them their first lesson of what it means to be an overcomer.

A well-known song by Bob Carlisle builds on this learning process: *We fall down, but we get up, we fall down but we get up.* Repeating for emphasis Bob continues, *We fall down, but we get up, for a saint is just a sinner who fell down!* The truth is, we all fall, and this fact underscores the reality that falling is a natural occurrence of life. We fall physically. We sometimes fall emotionally. We even fall spiritually and morally as well. However, falling is not the end. No matter what causes your fall, it's important to get back up again, since falling affirms one physical reality—anything that goes up will come down. Interestingly, and as revealed in the song, falling provides an interesting parallel with the construct of failure; however, with two distinctive responses. To the pessimist, failure defines a state; while to the optimist, failure represents an occurrence. That probably explains why when pessimists fall they often stay down, while on the other hand, when optimists fall, they view their failing as the result of a temporary misstep. Like optimists, overcomers view failure as a point in time—a random occurrence that results from a temporary misstep. Failure does not represent a state for the overcomer;

it simply makes a statement about their setback. Failure does not define the overcomer; failure simply refines them. While failure serves as a reminder that weakness exists, failure requires determined resolve to get back up, acknowledging the errors of the past, and resolving to move forward with renewed hope and opportunity.

In a twisted irony, failure is an essential ingredient for success. All successful individuals, and even organizations, have experienced failure at one

Failure is the canvas upon which success stories are written!

point or another. Take for example, Rovio Entertainment, the company that developed *Angry Birds*. Rovio developed fifty-one games before developing this well-known video game. Think for a moment what would have happened if Rovio's entire game development process was reduced to a one year (52-week) time span. The company would have only experienced success in the 52nd week—the last week of the year! Imagine the enormous development costs and hours of programming that were invested during the first fifty-one weeks with no sign of meaningful success. Despite their efforts, developers persisted in the midst of what seemed like certain failure. Then in the 52nd week, success strikes BIG, and *Angry Birds* 'slings' into the history books as one of the most successful video games in history. What would have happened if the developers gave up after the 10th attempt to develop this successful game? Surely they could have walked away after the 30th, 40th, or 50th attempt! But they did not. Failure did not define them; failure refined them! Similarly, Michael Jordan—one of basketball's greatest legends—also admits to failures. "I've missed more than 9000 shots in my career. I've lost almost 300 games. Twenty-six times I've been trusted to take the game winning shot and missed. I've failed over and over and over again in my life. And that is why I succeed." Failure is the canvas upon which success stories are often written. No matter your reason for falling, always remember that the overcomer is not defined by failure—he is refined by it. So the next time you are tempted to stay down after your next fall, remember that the overcomer is just a sinner who not only fell down, but someone who got up! Despite your failings, be encouraged that God's grace is still sufficient for you. Have faith in Him and give Him the chance to turn your mourning into laughter, and your failure into success.

Reflection: *Success is failure's lesson on resilience.*

12.

Faith

Chapter Goal: *Pray bold prayers today! Be anxious for nothing and make your requests known to God with thanksgiving.*

WHEN WAS THE LAST TIME you found yourself in one of life's turbulent storms that challenged your faith? How did you respond? Were you anxious, fearful, or hopeful? When confronted with life's obstacles, it's often easy to lose hope, or give up and throw in the proverbial towel. Unfortunately, some turn to drugs and other addictive substances chasing a high that never satisfies, while others, turn to their faith believing that greater is coming despite contradictory evidence. It is in these times of desperation when your faith is tested the most—the time when you need to look beyond the visible to a God who sees the invisible, trusting that He is in control of your situation.

The Oxford dictionary defines faith as "complete trust or confidence in someone or something." It is grounded in a belief system that often lacks empirical evidence, yet time and time again, it is proven through one's personal experience. Hebrews 11:1 provides a biblical perspective on faith, defining it as "the substance of things hoped for, the evidence of things not seen." Stated another way, faith is the certainty of the unknown when viewed through the prism of uncertain-knowns. Faith is tested in direct view of contradictory facts. Faith is challenged by the absence of evidence. Faith is rooted in an abiding confidence that knows that a solution is already in motion before the problem has even a chance to recognize its conclusion. Faith gives the assurance that the enemy of your circumstance has already been defeated. Faith gives God the opportunity to demonstrate His awesomeness by making the impossible possible.

In Hebrews 11:6, the Apostle Paul wrote, "without faith it is impossible to please him: for he that cometh to God must believe that he is, and that he is a rewarder of them that diligently seek him." Is it any wonder we often fail when we rely on our own strength, our own ideas, and our own strategies? Overcomers put their faith in God, knowing that when their will is surrendered to Him, He stands ready to act on their behalf. Faith in action, therefore, allows the overcomer to achieve that which seems impossible. Overcomers subject their will to God, reaching beyond their own comprehension to partner with a God who is beyond comprehension to achieve the incomprehensible.

One of the unique characteristics of faith is that it does not coexist with any of our natural senses. Duawne Starling once said, "If you can see it, taste it, hear it, smell it, or touch it, then it does not require faith." On his record *Deeper Faith*, Duawne's title track "If This Is Faith" describes his experience:

> **Faith is rooted in an abiding confidence that knows that a solution is already in motion before the problem has even a chance to recognize its conclusion**

In the valley, or mountain high, In the winter or mid July
I've decided to hold on tight, to what I believe inside
When I'm blinded with doubt and fear,

When I'm struggling to just be still
And the lesson is not quite clear, That's when I realize

If this is faith, I'm going deeper beneath the weight,
the weight of it all
And what should break me I end up breaking,
with every step I take, if this is faith

Like Duawne, overcomers must live with the assurance of their forthcoming promise in the face of contradictory evidence. Faith provides the assurance that your mountain will be made low, and your valley be converted into a refuge of safety. Faith provides the vehicle for the overcomer to go deeper, stand stronger, grow wiser, and ultimately experience God to the fullest.

Reflection: *Faith is likened to the size of a seed. Faith is nurtured by the power of God's word. Faith is harvested in the midst of the unseen.*

13.

Mountains & Valleys

Chapter Goal: *Confront the obstacles that stand in the way of achieving your dream.*

STANDING AT 29,029 FEET IN the Himalayan Mountains is the world's tallest mountain. Many experienced mountaineers have attempted to scale its rocky sides, some reaching its summit and others meeting their tragic end. It takes a special individual to plan, prepare, and attempt that cold death-defying hike that has claimed over 200 lives. Braving the dangers of altitude sickness, treacherous weather, high winds, and unpredictable avalanches, the thrill of conquering the heights of Mount Everest is often worth the climb.

But what is it about these tall, cold, and naked landmarks that inspire the dare-devil in us? Mountains challenge us to reach a higher place. Mountains force us to climb them to achieve a goal. Mountains cause us to risk everything in the pursuit of our dreams and goals. But mountains also have one unique characteristic: mountains always stand atop of a valley. Just as the summit of a mountain represents the highest measurable point of the mountain, the valley represents the lowest point of our experience. While coexisting in the same geographic space, mountains and valleys give also a unique glimpse into our sometimes bifurcated reality. For example, mountains stand tall above the fray. They receive the full force of nature at their summits, exposing their earthly skeletons. Despite their imposing figures, mountains often stand cold, frozen, and barren, lacking any sight of vegetation. On the other hand, valleys fall at the feet of mountains. Valleys collect water that flow first as tributaries, then streams, then rivers and then ultimately collects into large lakes. Valleys retain all the nutrients and rich soil that feeds the surrounding vegetation. Valleys provide food, shade, and safety for wildlife that live in its surrounding undergrowth.

Each of these contrasting parallels reflects important stages of our own pursuit for success. Everyone desires to climb the mountain of success, but after spending much effort scaling its steep sides—the sides of career, personal goals, and endearing aspirations—we finally reach the summit only to discover that the mountain top could be the loneliest place of one's existence. Our personal mountains may stand above the fray of those living in the valleys, but how often we become targets of the brute force of nature? Often exposed to the wind, rain, and snow, the mountains of our character, values, and relationships many times become the victim of our

> **Overcomers trust in the God who led Moses to the mountain while at the same time blessing His people in the valley.**

own success and abandonment. On the other hand, the valley provides shelter. God promises to be with you in the valley. He promises never to leave you nor forsake you. In the valley, He restores our souls. In the valley, He spreads green pastures before us that are filled with lush vegetation. In the valley, He provides springs of water that refreshes our soul.

The parallel between mountains and valleys may seem polarizing, and may even appear to discourage the pursuit and attainment of wholesome goals. However, when we realize that God is the mountain to whom we can run to and hide, the sooner we will recognize that He is truly our shelter in the time of storm. Overcomers abide in the presence of God, whether on the mountain or in the valley. They recognize that despite their lonesome walk in the valley, or being exposed to the elements on the mountain of success, God's loving presence always surrounds them.

Overcomers do not fear the mountain. Overcomers do not fear the valleys. Overcomers trust in the God who led Moses to the mountain while at the same time blessing His people in the valley. No matter your circumstance, remember that Your Heavenly Father promises to be with you. The question is: Do you trust Him to shield you while on the mountaintop or to shelter you while in the valley? Trust Him to create divine connections that unite your dreams, purpose, and passion with your destiny. Take God at His word and rest in the assurance that He will always be right by your side.

Reflection: *Mountains are conquered on step at a time.*

14.

Divine Connections: Part 1

Chapter Goal: *Walk humbly in your ability; place all your trust in God's capability!*

THE YEAR IS 1998, AND I am working as a computer technician for one of the largest computer firms in the country. There are a number of incidents and onsite repairs that compel my attention. The phone rings, and on the other end, is the managing director who calls me to his office. Mr. Benjamin briefs me on a call he received from the branch manager at the Canadian Imperial Bank of Commerce (CIBC) who reported that his accounting systems were unresponsive. Quickly, I retrieved my toolkit and rushed to the location to investigate the source of the issue. Upon my arrival, and as I made my way through the bank's security, I quickly sensed that my tall and lanky physique led some to question my ability to resolve the issue. I greeted the branch manager with a firm handshake and sat in his office to survey the issue. Within minutes I was able to isolate the cause of the issue and within the hour the computer system was back online. Later that morning, the branch manager called me into his office again, this time for a much different reason. Looking into my hidden potential, he asked: "Young man, what would you like to do with your life?" I thought this was a very insightful question and then responded, "Very interesting question, sir." Ten minutes into my answer it dawned upon me that there was much I wanted in life but was ill-equipped to achieve without help. Sitting across the table was a powerful person with influence and depth of relational connections that could change the trajectory of my life forever. And he did. You see, as I was speaking, he began writing the name of another important person whom he directed me to call. Unbeknownst to me, I had in my hand the name and direct number to the Director for the Organization of American States, Dr. Kenneth Jordan.

I returned to my desk with a sense of pride, reflecting on the job I just completed. I picked up the phone and dialed the number. After I introduced myself and stated the purpose of my call, Dr. Jordan agreed to meet with me. A few days later, I sat across the desk from another powerful, stately, and senior gentleman who described an educational program that he oversaw for the country. I listened intently as he described the competitive nature of the application process, entrance requirements, and the likelihood of being selected. I wondered to myself do I even stand a chance—considering that I had yet to prove myself academically. I left his office, somewhat bewildered, but thankful all at the same.

> **Divine connections may be clothed in the good deeds of others—notice them!**

Having just graduated with my Associates Degree in Electronics Engineering Technology, my clouds of doubt lifted after realizing that I did stand a chance to compete for a fully funded fellowship. I quickly reviewed all the information that Dr. Jordan provided and began compiling the list of documents to officially compete for this potentially life-changing opportunity.

Fast-forward a few months: My phone rings and on the other end is Dr. Jordan's executive assistant who advised me that Dr. Jordan has requested an audience with me. I immediately made myself available and rushed to his office. Upon arrival, I was handed a letter from the evaluation committee from which I learned that I was one of two recipients who won the chance of a lifetime—a fully funded scholarship to attend any US college or university to pursue an undergraduate degree in the field of Engineering! With tears running down my cheeks, I thanked God for His favor. I realized that my meeting the bank manager that day, and subsequently my meeting Dr. Jordan, was indeed a divinely appointed connection.

Sometimes, God places people in your path—people He chooses to use to connect you with your destiny. These divine connections eventually shape your future, instill wisdom, and challenge you to reach your greatest potential overcoming the obstacles that hold you back.

Reflection: *Your stature does not determine your capacity; your circumstance does not determine your destiny.*

15.

Divine Connections: Part 2

Chapter Goal: *Take time to notice the people God placed in your life to prepare you for your season of harvest.*

TIME PASSED SWIFTLY AND BEFORE long I was on the brink of completing four years of engineering study. I stood in line at the side of the stage waiting to hear my name called. "Graduating with a Masters in Administration, with an emphasis in Engineering Management is Donnell Josiah." That day I marched across the stage to receive a diploma with my name written on it—a diploma that some wondered if I would ever achieve. As I exited the stage, I said to myself, you did it Donnell! That day, receiving my diploma signaled to me that today, I am an Overcomer! With my family at my side, I held my head with overcoming pride knowing that I ran the race, I finished the course—a course set on the track that was God's design.

It wasn't long before I remembered the many nights I cried myself to sleep, frustrated by the difficult coursework of Calculus, Furrier Analysis, Transient Analysis, and other complex mathematical engineering maneuverings. It did not take long to realize that I stood on the shoulders of so many people who believed in me, including my Mom, Dad, siblings, and now my new bride. It didn't take long to remember the Peace Corp volunteer, Steven Wexler, who devoted his evening hours to assist me in dissecting equations that seemed to have been conceived in the pit of the underworld. It didn't take long to realize that God's timing leads us to connect with individuals along life's path; individuals who help us reach the summit of our destiny. These are divine connections that matter, and connections that last a lifetime.

Fast forward to 2002, and I have just relocated from

Andrews University to Maryland. The following day I was introduced to a middle-aged gentleman who I was told was a successful entrepreneur. After a very inspiring conversation, I handed him my resume. I received a call from Dr. Robert Wallace's executive assistant later that week requesting a meeting. This meeting resulted in my first job as an Engineering Manager at BiTHGROUP Technologies, followed by numerous subsequent consulting assignments and IT projects.

While working at BiTHGROUP, I developed an earnest love and respect for Dr. Wallace, his vision, and his entrepreneurial spirit. This admiration provided me a front seat at the feet of someone who had the ears of governors, mayors, and highly influential people

Divine connections may lay dormant in opportunities for self-advancement—get prepared and pursue them!

from across the State of Maryland. As a result of this divine connection, I developed an interest in starting my own consulting business, and years later, three entrepreneurial ventures were birthed. Each step of the way, God placed people in my life to guide me towards my purpose, much like the mile-markers at the side of the road. Each day He will do the same for you, but like overcomers, it is up to you to nurture the opportunities provided through God's divine connections.

Divine connections may be clothed in the good deeds of others—notice them!

Divine connections may be hidden through the help you provide someone in need— help as many as you can!

Divine connections may lay dormant in opportunities for self-advancement— get prepared and pursue them!

Divine connections are God orchestrated.

Divine connections are self-liberating.

Divine connections are divine!

God places people in your path each day; people who He chooses to use to connect you with your destiny. These divine connections eventually shape your future, instill wisdom, and challenge you to reach your greatest potential. In the end, divine connections enable you to move past obstacles, connecting you with your purpose, and ultimately your life's destiny. So take courage, God has not forgotten you. Stay connected to Him as he fulfills His promises for your life.

Reflection: *Your most sought after blessing may be camouflaged as an untimely inconvenience.*

16.

Courage

Chapter Goal: *Confront your fears and share your plan for achieving a life-goal with someone you trust.*

IT WAS JULY 21ST 1998. My ticket was purchased, my bags were packed, and I said my last goodbyes to some who I would never see again. My heart raced almost uncontrollably, fearing what this new chapter in my life will bring. It was difficult to push back the repressed thoughts that took root over several years— thoughts that were based on lies, and thoughts that left me feeling that I was never going to amount to anything in life.

Well, my time had come to leave the village of my

birth, a place where I created many memories. As I drove through the village, waving goodbye to my childhood friends, tears welled up in my eyes. I knew that my life would never be the same. As I stood on the steps of destiny I peered into the future—a future that God was about to share with me. On my way to the airport, I stopped by to say, "So long," to Aunt Rachel and Uncle Morris. As I was getting ready to leave, my dear uncle looked me in his eyes and with a deep conviction in his voice, he began to quote a passage taken from Joshua 1:9: "...Be strong and of a good courage; be not afraid, neither be thou dismayed: for the Lord thy God is with thee whithersoever thou goeth."

Suddenly, my fears were confronted with courage. Despair morphed into hope, and for the first time, I saw what others failed to have seen—the promise of becoming someone great! I began to realize that my time had come. My time came to shine, to reach for the stars, to become the go-getter that my Mom raised me to be. That time had come for me to lay hold of God's hand, and with courage, to move forward into my destiny. Sometimes the missing piece in the puzzle of life is courage. Courage is the catalyst that confronts fear, pain, danger, and uncertainty in the pursuit of your life's purpose. Courage is not the absence of fear, but the ability to triumph over it. Courage fuels the desire to bring about meaningful change. Courage awakens the dreams of purpose and challenges purpose to rendezvous with its destiny.

Think about your fears. Think about your goals of starting a business, raising a family, or completing that degree you never had a chance to finish. Think about **Courage is not the absence of fear, but the ability to triumph over it.** that life-changing decision that you still have not made—the decision that could potentially change the course of your life forever. Overcomers pursue their greatness outside by confronting their fears inside. Overcomers are not afraid to take action; rather, overcomers reach past the obstacles of today to chase the promise of their tomorrow. Overcomers place faith, hope, and trust in God believing that He will do that which He promised to do in their lives. Overcomers are courageous. Overcomers are risk takers. Overcomers may sometimes feel delayed, defeated, and afraid, but during these times, overcomers must confront their doubts, push past their fears, and move forward to conquer their dreams.

Reflection: *Courage is often confronted by fear, conflicted by defeat, but ultimately perseveres to victory.*

17.

Delayed,
Not Defeated

Chapter Goal: *Learn through the experience of others then take the plunge! Go ahead and register your business, commit to social change, pursue your dreams!*

ZERO! THAT WAS THE ANNUAL gross revenue for ChangeDynamix, the management consulting firm I founded seven years ago. Since then, it seemed like the odds were stacked against me and winning my first contract would be as easy as landing a rocket on the moon. Each year an obstacle presented itself, preventing me from taking the leap of faith into entrepreneurship. For seven years, I paid my annual fees to the State to keep the company open while watching other organizations build their practices on the strength of my credentials. For seven years, I updated the company's website advertising my consulting services to State governments. For seven years, I prayed for opportunities that all too often seemed destined for everyone except me. For seven years, I waited and seven years later, NOTHING!

Conflicted with a flurry of emotions wrapped in frustration, I had to confront the enemy of defeat. The enemy that often whispered, "Just close it all down, remove the website, expire your State registrations, and walk away from your seven years of hard work." But the overcomer in me roared back: "You are not a quitter, you are not a failure, and nothing will stand in the way of success when your steps are ordered by God." This was the inspiration I needed to continue chasing my dream. While I was still afforded gainful opportunities during this seven-year period, opportunities that mitigated the risks associated with owning my own business, I still needed to pursue the dream of owning and operating my own consulting business. However, during this period of drought, God was shaping me and preparing my fallow ground of inexperience for what was to come. Each day I worked even harder, using every opportunity to develop my entrepreneurial skills. At the same time God was placing individuals in my life, seasoned business owners who were able to teach me the 'ropes' of business ownership. What I did not realize was that my harvest was going to be preceded by a drought, and sure enough, I suddenly found myself in a dry

How can God bless your dream if you are busy building someone else's dynasty?

place of unemployment. It's as if God was saying to me, for the last seven years I prepared you to walk into your purpose, but how can I bless your dream if you are busy building someone else's? It slowly began to make sense. I began to see how God orchestrated opportunities that allowed me to lead some of my largest projects in my career, enabling me to build strong industry credentials. I also began to realize that God was developing my character as an overcomer through hard work, perseverance, and a clear sense of purpose. Overcomers pursue their purpose with passion and conviction, but overcomers must also sometimes go through the droughts of life so they can be prepared to receive their harvest. During my seven-year period of drought, God was actually grooming me to manage my own business, but I couldn't see it at the time. He allowed me the opportunity to develop strong business and technical acumen, leading some of the most visible web deployments for the US Government. He also provided me the opportunity to lead a complex portfolio of technology projects for the State of Maryland facilitating statewide educational reforms. These experiences prepared me for my harvest, and seven years later, that day arrived. Today, ChangeDynamix is a young and growing company that is now delivering management consulting services to the State of Maryland.

Overcomers are sometimes delayed in acquiring their dreams, but overcomers do not give in to defeat. Overcomers pursue their goals in the face of hardship and drought believing that one day they will reap the harvest of their hard work. Overcomers realize that while God may appear to delay His answers, His answers are never delayed. Overcomers keep fighting. Overcomers keep pressing forward believing that one day they will receive the blessings that God has promised. Do you feel delayed praying for a new job, a spouse, a new career, or to start a family? Hold on during this period of waiting, because like overcomers, your delay will be defeated when you rise and face today with conviction, taking hold of your purpose, and then walking into your destiny!

Reflection: *The road of life may be filled with bumps, detours, and setback. Never leave the path! Your dreams last only as long as your willingness to pursue them.*

18.

Rise, Take, Walk!

Chapter Goal: *Believe that He who is invisible can make the impossible possible!*

IT'S A COLD WINDY DAY on the path of the Beth Zeta Valley. The stench of dung is stifling from the nearby sheep market. He had nowhere to go. Like his other friends, he remained nameless, lacking the dignity of human identity in a culture that viewed his plight as a result of his own wrong doing. He was crippled and unable to walk; not only crippled by his infirmity, but crippled in his mind. Each day he sat at the edge of his circumstance hoping that his change would come, but for thirty-eight long years, he remained in the same location waiting for someone to assist in his miraculous deliverance. After what seemed to be a lifetime, he not only needed healing for his physical infirmity, but he needed healing for his broken and barren spirit. Confusion confronted his calamity, sadness sickened his spirit, and desperation deepened his doubt of ever being fully restored. But one day an unseen visitor asked him an unexpected question: "Wilt thou be made whole?"

Lifting his shoulders from his worn and fly-infested bed, he leaned forward in the direction of the one asking him the rhetorical question. Puzzled, he pondered sarcastically to himself, this man must be from the land of Crazy where Stupid is king! Taming his mental insults through his humble state of impotence, he explains to the unknown visitor that he has no help. No help to move him from a place of shame and illness. No help to lift him out of his place of abandonment. No help to break the chains that took his mind captive. No help to overcome what appeared as his certain death sentence. As he was about to blurt another reason for his pitiful condition, Jesus confronts his circumstance with a command: "Rise, take up thy bed, and walk!"

After thirty-eight years of bewilderment, the power

of Jesus' words carried three commands that would forever change his life. These same commands instruct overcomers today on how to live their lives.

Rise: This was a command that compelled action—action to move from the low place of self-crippling doubt to an elevated place of redeeming hope. It was a command to exercise immense faith, lifting him from the dusty ground that his frail body trampled for thirty-eight years. It was a command to overcome the imprisonment of his fears and the emancipation of his mind.

Take: This was a command to exert physical strength—strength that would be tested by his fear of failure and challenged by his infirmity. This was also a command to activate his faith and to take hold of his new future as a completely healed man. It was also a command to get up off the bed that insulated

> **Wilt thou be made whole? Rise, take up you bed, and walk into your day with the conviction knowing that the God of strength, and the God who never fails, has already promised you overcoming power!**

him from the downtrodden path and to walk freely into his destiny.

Walk: This was his command to act, to move forward, to make a decision confronting his fears. This was his command to walk away from friends who said your deliverance will never come and from an environment whose stench only reminded him of his rejected past. Walk! This is a command to put one foot ahead of the other in pursuit of his destiny. This was his divine invitation to become an overcomer, overcoming not only the obstacles of the past, but obstacles of his circumstance.

Overcomers are given the same commands. *Rise* with a renewed purpose, conviction, and hope of becoming the best you. *Take* hold of your faith, passion, and courage, and *walk* with the conviction knowing that He who has commanded you will give you the fortitude to *walk* into your destiny. Wilt thou be made whole? Rise, take up you bed, and walk into your day with the conviction knowing that the God of strength, and the God who never fails, has already promised you overcoming power.

Reflection: *Helplessness may be the state of one's emotion, but never should it become the state of one's condition.*

19.

Endearing Traits

Chapter Goal: *Focus on the things that you do best and leverage the skills of others to do the rest.*

MANY OF US DO FEW things well, but fewer of us do many things well. Is it through a stroke of genius, or are they simply wired for success? How do these individuals acquire the knowledge and expertise so as to be proficient in so many areas of life? On the other hand, there are many successful individuals who limit their focus by doing only a few things. Ironically, their focus on less seems to produce more! No matter which side of the spectrum you find yourself, one thing is certain: overcomers do not climb the ladder of success solely on their educational achievements, technical prowess, or stroke of luck; overcomers simply approach life differently. Understanding this difference is essential to extracting clues to their success, clues that offer a practical perspective on how we, too, can succeed. For example, overcomers set realistic **goals** and exercise concerted effort to meet these goals. Overcomers also know how to work smart and not hard, while **leveraging** their influence and their wider **team**. Overcomers are persistent, determined, driven, and focused. They are not easily deterred from accomplishing that which their mind is set to accomplish. These are not just unique characteristics of overcomers; these are what I call endearing traits, so let's take a closer look at each.

Goals: My mom used to say, "Aim high and reach for the stars, and if you fall, you will reach the moon." Admittedly, I never quite understood how to aim for the stars as a child. However, over the years, Mom's admonition stayed with me. I came to discover her emphasis was really not the attainment of impossible feats as landing on a distant star, but rather, on being intentional about setting personal goals, and doing everything within my power to accomplishing the same. This is one of the most important traits of the overcomer. Overcomers recognize that goal setting is crucial towards accomplishing their purpose. Goals inspire to action. Goals set direction. Goals fuel ambition. Goals compel attention. While long-term goals are effective strategic tools, short-term goals provide the most meaningful outcome for the overcomer. Short-term goals instill accountability and provide useful metrics for assessing success or failure. Short-term goals provide 'punctuated milestones' that help to create momentum towards accomplishing longer-term goals.

Teamwork: Teamwork is an essential enabler for success because goal attainment often requires the help of others. Overcomers enlist the help of others in their pursuit of success, not mainly out of a sense of dependence, but rather, through the shared interests, ambitions, and mutually beneficial goals that teamwork and collaboration afford. Overcomers also learn to create an inner circle of individuals based on their unique strengths—strengths that offset their own perceived areas of weakness. While their own personal talents are important, overcomers recognize the strength and collective wisdom that exists in working together. Michael Jordan once said: "Talent wins games, but teamwork and intelligence win championships."

> **Goals inspire action, set direction, fuel ambition, and compel attention!**

Teamwork wins games, but teamwork also provides the fortitude to enable overcomers to triumph over their obstacles.

Leverage: While overcomers may be able to do many things well, they also learn to exert time and effort only on the things they do best, and leveraging the skills of others they trust to do the rest. Leverage refers to the ability to exercise the most force with the least amount of effort. Leverage is the ability to exercise the force of influence so as to facilitate desired outcomes with the least amount of effort. Leverage is not to be confused with delegation. Delegation involves entrusting oversight and accountability to someone else to meet a specific goal. On the other hand, leveraging requires that you maintain accountability for the attainment of your desired goal, but work with those on your team to acquire your desired goal. Through leveraging the strength of others on their team, overcomers work smarter not harder. They build and nurture relationships so that truly 'Together they Each Accomplish More'— T.E.A.M.

Reflection: *Each person has a unique set of skills and strengths. Learn to tap into this valuable resource to produce outcomes that you cannot create on your own.*

20.

Persistence

Chapter Goal: *Identify three specific tasks that you would like to complete today. Dig deep and get it done!*

DESPITE MY BUSYNESS OF LIFE, I have often discovered that there is always something to do, and the moment when I think there is nothing else to do, it isn't long before I realize that there is indeed something else I must do. This somewhat twisted irony is often the reality for persistent people. Those who understand the value of hard work develop a work ethic that does not lose sight of their goals, and those who refuse to live aimlessly live with their goals in mind. Persistence does not relent. Persistence always drives you to go the extra mile, tugging at what my mom often called the 'go-getter spirit.' As kids, my Mom etched a poem into our brains that has now become my personal mantra even in my adult years. An excerpt from this poem, originally written by Susan M. Fenton Willoughby, states: "The go-getter goes till he gets what he goes for. The go-getter works till he reaps what he sows for. He fixes a goal and resolves when he sets it. The way to the prize is to go till he gets it."

Persistence and perspiration often make an unbeatable combination for success. One will argue that success cannot exist without this twin combination. Persistence is the tenacious drive to pursue a goal. Persistence does not give in, even when subjected to the weight of insurmountable pressure. Persistence does not give up, even when bombarded with life's obstacles. To the contrary, persistence pursues success at all costs believing that success is right around the corner. Persistence endures the pain of hardship knowing that ease and comfort often lead to disappointment. Overcomers press forward expecting that they will one day accomplish that which they have set out to achieve. Overcomers invest their sweat and tears in their pursuits, because the quality of their success is enhanced through the pain they had to endure to achieve it.

Success often requires sacrifice, but lasting success always requires persistence. Persistence is the fuel that ignites the go-getter spirit and opposes anyone who dares to hold you back from your destiny. Persistence channels focus towards the attainment of your life's goals. Persistence will challenge those who may attempt to quench your passion and potential. Persistence pursues your life's purpose and delivers it through the womb of hurt, pain, and rejection. Persistence says, "I can" when surrounding circumstances suggest "I can't." Persistence forces you to move forward until the prize that is to be won is achieved.

Persistence always rewards hard work with success.

When Usain Bolt sprinted past the potholes of his Jamaican village— Sherwood Content — and into the record books at the 2012 London Olympics, he exploded the cheers of his fans, but he also silenced the doubts of his naysayers. Growing up in a rural village with no streetlights and limited running water, he faced hard times. Bolt learned how to channel these hard times to his swift feet, and before long, his training paid off. Diagnosed at an early age as being hyperactive, his persistence insisted that he could be not just a great athlete, but the best! Today, with many world titles under his belt, Bolt has proven that persistence always rewards hard work with success.

Like Bolt, overcomers are persistent. Overcomers do not give up in the face of obstacles. Overcomers quiet the loud voices that attempts to silence their confidence. Overcomers listen to their inner giant that screams: "I can do it," "I am somebody," and "I will be all that God intends for me to be." Overcomers are reassured through Scripture that says: "I can do all things through Christ which strengthened me." Persistence compels action. Persistence requires that you keep pushing until you acquire that which you pursue. Persistence demands that you keep working until you reap what is sown. Just as in Mom's poem, overcomers set goals and resolve to attain them, because the way to the prize is the way to go until you achieve the prize. Don't give up. Don't give in. Pursue the dream that God placed deep within.

Reflection: *The path to your prize is through perseverance. Push through the limits and pursue your dream!*

21.

Balance

Chapter Goal: *Spend time with family; do something meaningful; invest in yourself!*

WE LIVE IN A FAST paced society with everything and everybody demanding our attention, not to mention the precious little that remains of our time. We have personal commitments, work assignments, church related activities, schoolwork, homework, housework, and for those of us who are married, the responsibilities of being a spouse. Is it any wonder so many people become overwhelmed with life and succumb to untimely deaths? Balance is not only an important goal to achieve; it is essential for your own survival.

When thinking about balance, the word homeostasis comes to mind. In scientific terms, homeostasis is the regulatory process by which biological systems maintain stability by adjusting to environmental conditions that are optimal for their survival. Stated another way, homeostasis is the process of maintaining balance in all areas of life despite competing demands. Balance is critical for survival since a change in one area often affects one or several other changes in other areas. This is probably what led to Newton's third law that states: "For every action, there is an equal and opposite reaction." Observe what happens when your body gets hot. You'll notice that it employs an internal regulatory system that produces sweat, ultimately providing a counter-balance to your body's increasing temperature. Take another example: consider what happens when you go on a strict diet to meet what seems to be an elusive weight goal. Often you constrict your diet only to drive your body into 'conservation mode,' ultimately slowing down your metabolism, and rendering your calorie-burning engine useless. Here is where we uncover one of life's most important lessons: homeostasis/balance is accomplished **in the midst** of life's competing forces, not through the absence of it.

Overcomers strive for balance in their pursuit of success since success requires effort, effort requires change, and change is the natural occurrence of life. Overcomers embrace the natural challenges that life throws their way, recognizing that success requires balancing competing priorities and obligations. Balance does not mean the absence of effort and it does not mean seeking a life of perpetual ease. Balance also does not promise comfort, nor does it guarantee success, but what achieving balance does is assist in compartmentalizing life's demands into bite-sized segments of purpose that later converges into the realization of your destiny.

Overcomers achieve balance by giving focus to all areas of life, not necessarily all at the same time, but all in time!

Dealing with life's demands and competing pressures require developing a process for achieving balance. It requires making time for the things that are important, including you! Living a balanced life also requires that you get enough sleep, find ways to reduce stress, and increase ways of sharing your time, space, and emotions with those you love.

Like you, overcomers rise each day to confront what seems like never ending pressures—pressures that do not want to subside nor offer the luxury of convenience. Life comes at us full force and we have to be prepared to handle it when it comes. That's why the only way to respond is not by retreating or running away, but by confronting each challenge with focused attention and establishing a list of daily priorities based on urgency, impact, and importance. While balance requires effort and planning, achieving it is a crucial skill for the overcomer. Overcomers learn to persevere in the face of competing priorities. Overcomers achieve balance by giving focus to all areas of life, not necessarily all at the same time, but all in time!

Reflection: *It's impossible to say yes to everybody at the same time without neglecting the most important person—You!*

22.

Focus

Chapter Goal: *Give attention to, and complete with excellence, the goals that you will pursue today.*

ONE OF THE THINGS I love about professional cameras is their ability to automatically create stunning images. Taking 'point-and-shoot' to a whole new level, these expensive gadgets make amateurs appear as award winning photographers in no time. One of the magical features that I really love is autofocus. Autofocus is the feature that allows the camera to automatically make the subject of the picture appear at its sharpest at what is called the focal point—the center of interest or activity. Similarly, each of us has the ability to bring to the center a singular interest or activity that leads to a specific outcome. This ability is called focus. Focus brings to the center one's primary object of interest, thought, and action. Focus requires effort. Focus directs action. Focus eliminates distractions and channels energy towards accomplishing personal goals. With focus, the unessential distractions of life are blurred out and the central subject—achieving your life's purpose—move towards the focal point.

I have discovered that I sometimes spend a lot of time on activities that are not essential to helping me reach my full potential. But I am not alone! We all are bombarded with daily distractions that ultimately deter us from taking meaningful action necessary for accomplishing our goals. While some of these distractions are arguably unavoidable, many can be minimized, freeing up valuable time to pursue meaningful outcomes. With the rise of social media in the last few years, take a moment and reflect on how much time you spend tweeting and reading mindless updates of 'friends' you don't even know. Think about the many events you have attended that ended up being a colossal waste of time. Overcomers recognize that to fulfill their life's purpose, they have to eliminate distractions that deter them from attaining the goals they have set. They invest in themselves and commit to pursuing activities that only produce meaningful results—the acquisition of their destiny.

When I think about some of life's distractions, I think about my own love for electronics. Doesn't it seem like just a few years ago when computers, smart phones, and tablets were considered novelty items? Today, these modern techno gadgetries infiltrate almost every area of our lives. While their benefits are incontrovertible, the increased amount of electronic stimulation has made it almost impossible for individuals to focus on one thing. That's why overcomers must often unplug, get away, and disconnect from the world to bring into view that singular thought, action, or activity of importance. Overcomers reflect on what's important, take time to connect with friends and family, invest time in productive work, and spend time pursuing their own success.

> **Overcomers point to their future and shoot their best portrait by adjusting life's aperture, bringing into focus that one thing—the acquisition of their destiny.**

While it is unlikely that interest in these electronic

modern marvels will subside, one thing is certain: where focus goes, energy flows. Overcomers learn to focus on what's important by placing the many daily distractions that compete for their attention in their proper perspective. Overcomers channel their energy, passion, and focus on pursuing activities that result in meaningful outcomes. Overcomers dream big dreams, work hard, and pursue excellence, shooting the portraits of life in 'manual mode.' So while life for the overcomer may never exist in autofocus mode, overcomers *point* to their future and *shoot* their best portrait by adjusting life's aperture, bringing into focus that one thing—the acquisition of their destiny.

Today, make the choice to make a difference. Cultivate an attitude that eliminates distractions and those activities that do not produce meaningful results. Learn to say, NO, with the same smile with which you say, YES. Focus on what is important. Focus on who is important. Focus on igniting your true potential that today may still be entombed in your unrealized dreams. Reach, dig deep, and place yourself in position to chase your destiny with focus, purpose, and conviction.

Reflection: *Distractions come in all forms. It's essential to keep in view the things that will enable you to achieve your goals, realize your dreams, and ultimately achieve your destiny.*

23.

Be In Position

Chapter Goal: *Spend time developing, investing in, and building your unique brand so that you will be in position when opportunity knocks.*

SUCCESS IS OFTEN VIEWED IN terms of one's ability to perform. While this is partially true, success is really the combination of three critical elements: (a) preparation, (b) opportunity, and (c) positioning. Preparation includes developing the necessary competencies—knowledge, skills, abilities, and behaviors— to master that which you are attempting to succeed at. Opportunity is the blend of timing and circumstances that allows you to leverage your competencies in the pursuit of a desirable goal.

Positioning unites competencies with opportunity at a precise point in time that maximizes your ability to take advantage of an opportunity. So success really requires being prepared with the necessary skills and being in the right place at the right time!

In developing a plan for success, it is important to note that there are elements that are within your control and others that are not. For example, you can control your preparation by actively pursuing knowledge, improving your skills, developing technical abilities, and fostering purpose-driven behaviors. However, it's almost certain that if you fail to prepare, you will be ill-equipped to take advantage of available opportunities. This is true even if you may be in position to be considered for available opportunities. This results in missed opportunities, unrealized dreams, unmet goals, lack of personal and/or professional advancement, amongst several others. To capitalize on opportunities for advancement, overcomers spend time investing in their own personal development. This investment of time and resources is crucially important to prepare for success. So whether you are seeking success on the job or success in attaining a lifelong goal, remember that success often waits at the intersection of preparation and opportunity. The overcomer, therefore, must spend time pursuing knowledge, building new skills, and deepening their technical abilities. The overcomer must cultivate an attitude that allows them to pursue life with a sense of expectancy, anticipating opportunities before they are manifested. The overcomer does not wait until the opportunity presents itself to begin his preparation; rather, the overcomer lives by a playbook that requires him being in position at the right time to receive his blessing.

> **Success waits at the intersection of preparation and opportunity.**

To illustrate, I will use the analogy of a football team. There are several positions on a football team; however, there are two positions on the offensive line that intrigue me and often influence the outcome of the game. These two positions are the quarterback and the receiving positions. The quarterback is the most important offensive position. He communicates frequently with members of the coaching staff and relays the upcoming play to the team. Quarterbacks train hard. Quarterbacks study the playbook. Quarterbacks know precisely where to throw the ball even **before** the receiver is in position to receive the ball. Receivers are critical to the play as well. Their main job is to catch the ball at a precise location and time so as to avert an interception. Through their grueling training routines, receivers are prepared to run the play that is called by the quarterback. Like quarterbacks, receivers train hard. Receivers not only practice speed, but receivers practice specific run patterns that prepare them to catch the ball at the precise point, time, and location after the ball has been thrown.

It's game day and seconds after the quarterback pistols the ball through the air, the receiver maneuvers himself from around his defenders, takes his position, and prepares to snatch the ball of opportunity flying through the air. He turns, looks, and spots the ball as it rockets mid-air toward him. At the precise time and location he snatches the ball mid-air and sprints towards the end-zone for a touchdown. The same is true in the game of life. The quarterback has already thrown the ball filled with opportunity and promise for your success. As the receiver, it's your turn! It's up to you to break-free from the defensive tackles that hold you back, sprint into position, and snatch the blessings of opportunity that God has thrown in your direction. It's your decision; the ball of opportunity has been snapped and is now airborne. Go! Run for your touchdown!

Reflection: *You cannot control opportunity, but you can control your preparedness for it.*

24.

Decisions

Chapter Goal: *Make the decision to pursue happiness, and to be the best that you can be. Don't wait: Just Do It!*

ONE OF THE MOST RECOGNIZED logos in the world is the *Nike* swoosh. Resembling a curved check mark, the swoosh can be seen on sportswear items throughout the sporting industry, instantly instilling confidence in anyone wearing the brand. With annual revenues in excess of 25 billion, *Nike* stands as a formidable giant, commanding incredible brand awareness, market presence, and dominating the sports merchandising industry for decades. Equally distinctive, however, is its slogan. This simplistically profound three-worded slogan, "Just Do It," has inspired a generation of athletes, compelling action, persistence, drive, and countless victories. The slogan means more than just lacing up a pair of Nike sneakers or slipping into their matching set of neon colored outerwear. "Just Do It" means more than simply looking cool as you stride across the mall showing off the company's emblem of success. The slogan is intended to compel action, inspire change, and provoke your inner self to get on the move. For the athlete, the slogan is a charge for victory: a charge to train harder, run faster, swim longer, or just push harder until victory is reached.

Everyone is confronted with decisions; decisions about where to go to school, which job to take, which career to pursue, who to marry, amongst a host of other things. Decisions are intersections along the road of life that provide access to opportunity. Decisions are valleys that lie between the mountains of thought and action. Decisions are normal occurrences in life and are often clothed with consequences. Making right decisions often lead to happiness, while making wrong decisions often lead to anxiety, stress, and disappointment. That's why making decisions should never be trivialized as thoughtless random occurrences, but rather approached with careful thought, taking into consideration facts, opportunities, and consequences. Overcomers take decision-making seriously since they realize that their success may very well be contingent upon the decision they made previously, or the decisions that they are confronted in making today. Sometimes, overcomers are also confronted with the decision to break negative generational cycles in pursuit of meaningful actions that lead to restoration, life change, and ultimately long-term happiness. Overcomers decide to set meaningful goals that ultimately shape their future, leading to a more successful and rewarding life.

Decisions are valleys that lie between the mountains of thought and action.

On the other hand, while decision-making requires careful thought, it can also become quite a paralyzing exercise for others. This condition, often referred to as 'analysis paralysis,' causes individuals to over-think and over-analyze decisions to the extent that decisions are significantly delayed, and in some cases, never made. The decision-making process is, therefore, paralyzed through indecision resulting in missed opportunities. The overcomer avoids indecision since indecisions are themselves decisions to not make a decision. So while effective decision-making requires careful consideration of facts, opportunities, outcomes, and consequences, the overcomer resists the urge to over-analyze opportunities that could lead to paralysis. Rather, they engage in a series of steps that ultimately lead to action. They do this by developing a clear understanding of the nature of the decision to be made, along with its opportunities and consequences. They purposefully seek out information and consider available facts, since it's impossible to make sound decisions with unknown facts. They prayerfully filter these facts through their personal, moral, and ethical filters, while seeking the counsel of trusted friends to ensure that all facets are being considered. Once all these inputs are considered, overcomers then take action! Philippians 4: 6 and 7 admonishes the overcomer to "…be anxious for nothing, but in everything by prayer and supplication, with thanksgiving, let your requests be made known to God; and the peace of God, which surpasses all understanding, will guard your hearts and minds through Christ Jesus." So, like overcomers, make the decision, today, to lace up your proverbial *Nike* sneakers, slip into your matching *Nike* outwear, and pursue the dreams and goals with the "Just Do It" attitude. Don't procrastinate, make a decision and pursue happiness. Just Do It!

Reflection: *Decisions are choices that are accompanied by consequences. Make your choice matter.*

25.

Procrastination

Chapter Goal: *Avoid making excuses. Take one step toward becoming a better you today!*

AM I WHERE I AM supposed to be in life financially, emotionally, academically, or spiritually? If not, why? What am I putting off today, that if I only invest just a few minutes each day, will bring me one step closer to the life that I desire? Given that the best step towards getting something done is to simply begin, it's time to take action, so let's deal with the issue of procrastination head-on.

Procrastination is a fancy term that describes the tendency to put off important activities for a later time, and often in lieu of enjoying more pleasurable activities in the present time. It is a complex psychological behavior that affects everyone to some degree. For some, procrastination has become a perfected habit; a habit of waiting, delaying, or putting off important decisions, inevitably resulting in missed opportunities, unnecessary setbacks, and unfortunately, delayed personal development. For others, procrastination can lead to more severe outcomes, including stress, and anxiety, and other psychological disorders. So while it might appear as an innocuous act, procrastination can actually make life much more difficult by making an easy task unnecessarily difficult, and more difficult tasks, almost impossible.

Procrastination exists within a dangerous psychological cycle of self-deception. The procrastinator delays an activity believing that sufficient time is available, and thinking that everything is under control. Before long, the deadline looms resulting in a frantic rush to the finish line, albeit sometimes with sub-par results. The cycle continues, especially if the habit is rewarded, creating a more debilitating cycle. For example, you delay starting that important project that your boss assigned to you three weeks earlier. It's due in four days and you have not even begun the research. You rush to complete the project working 14-hour days, not only sacrificing your quality of life, but also sacrificing your professional credibility as a result of producing substandard work. While you are able to complete the project, it is a far cry from your best work. Not only do you know it, your colleagues and superiors also know it. What would have been the outcome had you planned, paced yourself, and executed assigned activities? On a broader scale, where would you have been today had you taken the necessary steps for your own growth five years ago? Procrastination ruins your future because you delayed yesterday what should have been completed today, risking your success tomorrow.

Procrastination robs because you delayed yesterday what should have been completed today, risking your future success tomorrow.

Procrastination does not help personal achievement, nor does it aid in the pursuit of personal and/or professional advancement. In fact, procrastination has been linked to a number of negative psychological associations such as depression and other forms of irrational behavior. In some cases, procrastination can become so debilitating, that it may require the intervention of a mental health professional. While most procrastinators do not require this degree of treatment, the habit can be beaten.

All through life we must make decisions; some lead to positive rewards and others sometimes result in regret. However, one thing is certain, consequences always follow actions, and to those who procrastinate, delayed actions and even indecision inevitably inflict setback, unnecessary stress, and unwanted anxiety. The good news is that procrastination can be defeated. It starts with one decision—the decision to take action today. Overcomers take action today to pursue their destiny. Overcomers fulfill their purpose not by watching others excel and advance in their lives, but by taking ownership of their lives. Overcomers accept responsibility to find and pursue their purpose. Overcomers resist the urge to make excuses for their circumstances. Overcomers avoid putting off today's challenge for tomorrow's reward. Overcomers do not make excuses; rather, they take responsibility, make decisions, and take the steps necessary to achieving their dreams.

Reflection: *Procrastination delays future happiness, inflicts unnecessary setback, and ultimately sabotages your ability to reach your full potential.*

26.

Responsibility to Forgive

Chapter Goal: *Forgive, as you would like to be forgiven.*

ONE OF THE MOST DIFFICULT experiences to overcome is childhood abuse. The emotional pain and mental scarring that result often lead to decades of anguish for some, and for others, leave deep wounds that sometimes never actually heal. Confronting the emotional pain of yesterday often requires reliving painful memories today, causing some to live with hatred and unforgiveness way into the future. This is true for individuals, but it is also true for ethnic groups that have been subjugated to atrocities that have lasted for several decades. The unfortunate reality is the dark past of oppression often obscures the hope for reconciliation—especially when current societal issues are reminiscent of past injustices. Without question, physical and emotional pain is difficult to forgive, but how long shall the memories of the past prevent you from reaching the promise of your future? On a broader scale, when will we begin to soothe the wounds of oppression with the ointment of forgiveness so that we can truly avail ourselves with the promise for a brighter tomorrow? Overcomers acknowledge the pain of yesterday and confront memories that may still reveal open wounds. However, overcomers are committed to taking the necessary steps forward—steps towards healing, reconciliation, and restoration.

Oprah Winfrey, having suffered childhood rape at the delicate age of nine, and becoming a teenage mother at the age of fourteen, offered a sobering reminder for the need to take responsibility. During one of her Master Class segments, Winfrey states:

"You are responsible for your life, and if you are sitting around waiting for someone to save you, to fix you, to even help you, you are wasting your time, because only you have the power to take responsibility to move your life forward. What matters is now, this moment, and your willingness to see this moment, for what it is, accept it, forgive the past, take responsibility and move forward."

Winfrey's admonition does not excuse wrongful action; rather, it challenges the overcomer to alter mental processes by channeling their energy towards healing and restoration. It also challenges the overcomer to take personal responsibility for their thoughts and actions, forcing them to look forward versus backward. Implicit in Winfrey's segment is the sobering invitation to extend forgiveness to individuals whose actions may have been injurious, and to commit oneself to thinking and acting differently in spite of the memories of hurt and pain.

Overcomers are committed to take the necessary steps forward; steps towards healing, reconciliation, and restoration.

Eleanor Roosevelt once said that a person's philosophy is not best expressed through words, but rather expressed in the choices they make. All through life the overcomer is confronted with decisions—

some that lead to positive rewards and others that sometimes result in regret. However, overcomers choose to make their tomorrows better than their today, recognizing that they are heirs of their decisions and actions. Overcomers embrace that fact that being responsible for actions and decisions imposes a social obligation to follow-through, to take ownership for themselves, and to pursue actions that result in the betterment of themselves and their families. Overcomers rise to the challenge and accept the responsibility to pursue their destiny while resisting the urge to make excuses for their circumstances.

Like overcomers, choose to take responsibility for your own actions since it represents the degree to which you can be trusted to do what is required, committed, and expected. Make the conscious decision to align your emotions with words, words with meaning, and meaning with actions, making for yourself a better and brighter tomorrow.

Reflection: *Forgiveness liberates love; un-forgiveness entombs hate.*

27.

Forgiveness of a Dreamer

Chapter Goal: *Reach for the stars! Dream big dreams today.*

HE WAS AN IMMIGRANT. HE looked different, spoke with an accent, and came from a large family. He dreamed big dreams. He had a bright future ahead of him, but what he did not realize was that his life was about to be turned upside down. At seventeen years old he is hanging out with his half-brothers who were up to nothing good. As they are herding sheep in the countryside, he slips away to report their misdeeds to his father. Already at odds with his brothers because of his father's favor, he was hated, talked about, and soon to be plotted against. One day while out in the fields, he shared the interpretation of one of his dreams with his brothers. Quite agitated, they scoffed at the absurdity of him becoming somebody great, but as he continued dreaming big dreams, envy quickly turned to hatred in the hearts of his brothers. At the request of his father, Joseph finally tracks down his brothers in the neighboring city of Dothan. To his surprise, his brothers were waiting, but waiting to destroy him. They stripped him of his possessions and abandoned him in an empty pit before selling him for twenty pieces of silver. Joseph will soon realize that the pit was God's pathway to his purpose.

Joseph arrives in Egypt on Pharaoh's fully loaded caravan destined to become a slave. As he arrives in the city he realizes that his predicament is very different from what he had dreamed. Standing on the trading block of slavery, the bid for his life goes higher and higher. With a shout, the auctioneer slams his hammer on the desk, "Sold to the gentleman in the corner." Joseph is released to his master, Potiphar, but deep inside he knew that God was with him. Each day as he worked in the fields, the hot sun scorching his back, he remembers who he was versus who he was sold to be. Joseph was an overcomer enslaved by the misdeeds of his family. However, despite his enslavement, Joseph refused to sacrifice his work ethic that was instilled in him from his land of birth. Before long, his work ethic paid off as his master—Potiphar—began to notice the quality of his work. Like overcomers, Joseph set daily goals and achieved them. He was passionate about excellence, and exerted discipline in its pursuit. He was consistent and successful at everything he put his hands to.

However, Potiphar's wife saw more than youthful passion, diligence, and persistence; she saw a handsome carving of masculine chocolate of which she wanted a

> **Overcomers forgive, not because it's easy, but because it's necessary.**

piece. After dusting her smooth skin with her most seductive fragrance, she waited for the right time to seduce him; but, before she could raise his testosterone levels, he fled leaving his clothes in her hands. Now wrongly jailed for being right and dishonored for honoring his master's bed, Joseph now awaited the lynching of his destiny. As time passed, the purity of his innocence was revealed to the warden, and before long he was entrusted to keep watch over the very prison that entrapped him. The prison of social injustice that was meant to squander his dreams now became the platform on which his best work would now be on display. The prison of lies that attacked his character now became the place where the King's dreams would be interpreted.

Like other dreamers, Joseph dreamed of the day when social injustice will be no more. He dreamed of the day when people from all walks of life will walk hand in hand. He dreamed of the day when his people would not be judged by the color of their skin but rather by the content of their character, and that day came. That day came when King's (MLK) dream was realized. That day came when equal opportunity was afforded to everyone willing to work hard. That day came when his oppressors came looking for food, and he finally disclosed his identity and offered them forgiveness. That day came when he ascended from the pit, above Potiphar's prison, and then was promoted to being President over the country. Overcomers forgive, not because it's easy, but because it's necessary. Overcomers free their oppressors from the indictments of their past, thus, freeing the overcomer to pursue his purpose with passion, confidence, and dignity.

Reflection: *Extending forgiveness may not be easy, but what forgiveness offers is the ability to free yourself from a place of bondage, liberating you into a place of freedom.*

28.

YOU-nique

Chapter Goal: *Embrace the fact that you are different, and it is this difference that makes you one-of-a-kind!*

THE *MONA LISA* IS ARGUABLY the most familiar piece of painting in the world. Painted by Leonardo da Vinci, the *Mona Lisa* made its debut on white Lombardy poplar panel in the early 1500s, and to this day remains an iconic work of art. What's equally interesting to the painting is the biography of its painter. Though Leonardo da Vinci was known as a skilled scientist, inventor, and doctor, he was still able to become arguably the most recognized artist in the world as a result of his work. Over the past 500 years, the *Mona Lisa* has begun showing its age; however, the mystique that inspired numerous writers, poets, and musicians over the centuries, continue to inspire contemporary works even through today. Despite the attempts of vandalism, thefts, and even cloning of the enigmatic smile, there remains today only one original copy of the *Mona Lisa*.

Now, take a look at you. What does your canvas show? Does it show a cheap imitation of someone else's portrait, or does it show a unique painting of someone destined for greatness? Does it show your value system acquiescing into something you are not, or does it put on display someone who is proud of your unique difference? You are the best and only version of you! You cannot be cloned, you cannot be duplicated, and 'all of you' are represented as your best contribution to humanity. Some may criticize you. Some may compare you to someone or some other standard, but in the end, you are all that is left when the lights go off. Love you! Build you! It's up to you to pursue the dreams and goals that will enable you to realize your unique purpose, and to allow you to reach your true destiny.

Overcomers are unique people. They recognize that despite their failings and shortcomings, their uniqueness is a distinguishing personal characteristic.

Overcomers embrace their difference knowing that they are 'one of a kind.' Overcomers are true to their individuality and possess the courage to stand alone. They are comfortable being different because they know that their contributions will create lasting impact and provide unique solutions to real world problems.

You are the best and only version of you!

Richard Smallwood was viewed as someone ahead of his time. Despite his musical abilities, he was told that his music didn't sound like everyone else's; that his music would not sell; and ultimately, that he would not make it in the music business. After graduating from Howard University with degrees in both vocal performance and piano, followed by his graduate work in ethnomusicology, Smallwood faced many challenges. Despite these challenges, Smallwood survived the odds and has since enjoyed a successful career in music lasting over four decades. Today, Smallwood's unique ability to fuse classical progressions with intricate Gospel harmonies has made him a household name. On his last record *Anthology*, Smallwood joined forces with Warren Shadd, an iconic piano manufacturer and the first African American piano manufacturer. For a moment, the past was eclipsed with the future as two icons with two great legacies shared one stage. The unique collaboration between Smallwood and Shadd will go down in history as the time when two legends created one history.

Despite your own opinions of you, it's time to start loving the 'you' that God made you to be. If you are an eagle, fly! If you are an instrument, create the best music ears will ever hear. If you are a sermon, preach like you have never preached before. If you are a portrait, display the beauty that radiates from inside. If you are simply you, then be you, love you, and become all that you were destined to be. Overcomers value their uniqueness, being true to themselves, their values, and their individuality. Overcomers do not bow to the pressures of mainstream society. So, be proud of your uniqueness and take every moment and enjoy the most important gift God gave when He made you, which is you!

Reflection: *What matters most is not the brush that is used on your canvas, but the unique image that the artist creates.*

29.

The Butterfly

Chapter Goal: *Cultivate relationships that facilitate positive life-changing transformations.*

AS I LOOK BACK OVER my life, it is clear that I have benefited from the guidance of the unseen hand of God. Through each of my trials, I can recount the many times I have seen God's deliverance and providence, and I have experienced His abiding presence. Many times I erred in my faithlessness wondering if my circumstances would ever turn in my favor. Yet, time and time again, I witnessed how the moving pieces of my circumstances were positioned by God to help me become an overcomer. I overcame the hurt that followed what appeared to some as a dismal showing of academic wit. I overcame the disappointment for not meeting the expectations of those who thought I was smarter than my grades proved. But now, some twenty-five years later, I clearly see that the struggle was meant to squeeze me from the cocoon that entrapped my purpose and potential. I have witnessed the unseen hand of God guiding me, connecting me to people, places and things—all being used to make me the person I am today. My transformation from being the lanky boy from a small rural village to now a budding philanthropist, entrepreneur, and consultant confirms that since I have overcome, so can you.

Stop! Take a moment and look yourself in the mirror. Observe the potential that is staring back at you. You become what YOU think you are! When you believe in yourself and think positive ennobling thoughts—even when those around you say otherwise—there is nothing you can't achieve.   Are you facing hardship? Probably, yes. Are you afraid of rejection or failure? Most of us are. But God has promised that if you connect your faith with your actions, victory is assured. Will it require work? Absolutely, but with the same resolve. I offer you the assurance that with a little effort each day, that your future may just be waiting for you on the other side of your fears. So what is your excuse for not trying? What is keeping you back? Trust the unseen hand of a loving God who is waiting to bless you immeasurably. While His blessings are assured, you have an important part to play in this transformation: you have to take the first step of faith. Overcomers must persist. Overcomers must persevere in the face of struggle. Overcomers must resolve within themselves to live a life that is fueled with determination, propelled by passion, and one that allows them to soar on the wings of faith in the pursuit of their destiny.

Your future may just be waiting for you on the other side of your fears!

Consider the metamorphosis of a butterfly. With over twenty thousand species, each adorned with their unique blend of radiant colors, each butterfly must confront death on its path to life. The butterfly must encounter death of the caterpillar that served as the surrogate of its destiny. The butterfly must confront death in the cocoon that trapped its wings, before falling away in view of a brighter future. Like the butterfly that is on its way to a new life, the overcomer must experience transitions that take place first in the heart. New desires must be birthed and new friendships must be cultivated. Like the butterfly, you must develop your new pair of antennae to receive the sensory impulses from your environment. You must develop your own legs to stand on, and your own pair of eyes to see the future that God has prepared just for you. Like the butterfly, you, too, must develop a whole new digestive system that no longer feeds on plant material, but on the sweet nectar of success. The transformation of the butterfly is nothing short of a miracle, and so will your transformation be as well. The overcomer digs deep and pushes past the death of its past.

The miracle for your metamorphosis is about to happen. It's your turn to fly. It's your turn to emerge from the cocoon of safety and launch into the promise of your future. It's your turn to show to the world the awesome and wonderful gifts that God has entrusted to you. Don't let someone else claim your spot at the finish line; the victory lap is yours to run. Go get it! Spread your wings and fly. YOU are a beautiful butterfly.

Reflection: *Change may not be easy, but transformative change is always necessary!*

30.

Moving Forward

Chapter Goal: *Learn from your failures. Celebrate your victories. Pursue your dreams!*

IT'S ALMOST MIDNIGHT AND MY family and I are driving home after a full day of ministry. We're tired, hungry, and craving some well deserved rest. The narrow road is dark, meandering for miles through small neighborhood towns. Approximately thirty minutes into the three-hour drive, we are all alone on this dark country road before running into some unexpected traffic. In front of us was a large fuel delivery truck that blocked our view of the road. Driving on this one-lane highway seemed like an eternity as my headlights reflected off the truck's long shiny fuel tank. I continued painfully slow for almost ten miles before realizing that the one-lane highway turned into two lanes! It wasn't long before I realized that I could have been much further along had I been just one lane over. After changing lanes, a clear open roadway stretched out before me. That night, I learned an important lesson: Sometimes to move forward in life, you must change lanes!

A well-known song by Israel Houghton talks about moving forward. 'Moving forward' carries a double directive: to **move** and to **go forward**. *Movement* is focused action, attention, and activity that is directed towards achieving a particular goal, while *forward* is the change in position that results in improved placement relative to your desired goal. Desirable movement results in positive, restorative, and regenerative outcomes. It can also ignite change, bringing important issues into focus. However, movement does not assure nor prescribe direction, since it is possible to move either forwards or backwards relative to your desired position in life. Despite occasional setbacks, overcomers focus their attention on moving forward. They focus their energies on pursuing meaningful activities that produce sustainable outcomes that align with their goals.

Moving forward is not only a directive; it is also a charge. Moving forward is a charge to think differently, to act differently, and to care for a humanity that is seemingly stricken with hopelessness and often with an obscured view of objectivity. Moving forward also involves personal ambition, goal setting, soul-searching, accountability, and self-reflection. It is a charge to place importance on values rather than valuables, and to be producers of creative solutions versus consumers of ideas that perpetuate societal decadence. Moving forward demands that we rise out of our valleys of despair and confront behaviors that sag beneath our waists, actions that are hooded in violence, and tendencies that are disguised

Sometimes in order to move forward in life, you must change lanes!

through generational entitlement. Moving forward acknowledges social injustice wherever it occurs and challenges us to love, live, and work with people who may appear different to us. Moving forward insists on racial reconciliation and the commitment to heal the gaps of pain and oppression that has separated cities all across this great nation. Moving forward challenges us to prioritize and passionately pursue our dreams and goals in search of our purpose.

When we make the effort to move forward, we commit ourselves to taking the important steps towards overcoming personal, cultural, and institutional obstacles that only serve as a wedge to divide us. When we move forward, we are able to walk hand in hand, not being afraid of our differences but embracing them believing that one day we as a community, people, and a nation will be free—free from the oppressive past that was wrought through slavery, and free from the depressive present that attempts to rob every opportunity from our future. While overcomers may occasionally look back over their lives to gain a clear appreciation for whence they have come, overcomers continually look ahead, committing themselves to meaningful activities that produce sustainable outcomes for themselves and the communities they serve. Overcomers accept the charge of Martin Luther King Jr. who said, "If you can't fly then run; if you can't run then walk; if you can't walk then crawl; but whatever you do you have to keep moving forward." Overcomers keep pressing forward believing that their past is over, all things are made new, and through God's help resolve to keep pressing, fighting, and moving forward until they reach their goals!

Reflection: *Your future exists on the other side of your fears.*

31.

Victory

Chapter Goal: *Finish your race with integrity and dignity!*

VICTORY IS OFTEN VIEWED AS an act of defeating an enemy, an opponent, or a system in a battle, game, or other competition. Victory can also be defined as the state of overcoming an obstacle in the pursuit of a goal. It is almost impossible to have a discussion about overcoming without providing the reassurance of victory. While achieving a gold medal, a coveted crown, or a first place position is important, it is more important to complete that which you have set out to achieve.

In the first sequel of Pixar's animated *CARS* movie, Lightning McQueen plays the lead role as a fast rookie race car that is driven to succeed. The movie begins with the last race of the Piston Cup championship, which lands the rookie race car in a three-way tie with two retiring veterans—Strip Weathers and Chick Hicks. To prove their track supremacy, the Piston Cup Championship race is scheduled as a tiebreaker. McQueen is all revved up and ready to compete against these two seasoned pros both of whom have an equal desire to win. As McQueen journeys across the country, he suddenly finds himself unexpectedly detoured on Route 66 before arriving in a small town of Radiator Springs. There, he gets to meet some new friends, one of which included Doc Hudson, known to many as the infamous 1951 Hudson Hornet. The plot thickens as McQueen is arrested and impounded. Desperate to leave town and reconnect with his team, the judge sentences McQueen to hard labor that involved resurfacing the town's main road. The judge will later go on to teach McQueen important techniques needed to master the course, since he was actually a three-time Piston Cup winner.

The Piston Cup Championship is here, and it's time for McQueen to prove his skills on the track. The countdown begins and suddenly these competitive die-hards zoom across the starting lane. Before long, McQueen finds himself in last place. With almost certainty of losing the race, McQueen hears the voice of his trainer, Doc Hudson, as he takes over as his crew chief. With a new sense of purpose, McQueen quickly emerges ahead of the pack to lead the race into the final laps. Desperation turns catastrophic as Chick Hicks now facing certain loss sends Strip Weathers into a dangerous spiral causing him severe injury. With victory in sight, McQueen makes the split decision to slam on his brakes after remembering that Doc Hudson also suffered a similar fate. With tires screeching, McQueen stops just short of the finish line. Hicks zooms past and crosses the finish line to win the race. The crowd gasps in wonderment completely befuddled as they now witness a sudden turn of events. McQueen drives over to the disabled veteran that lay vanquished on the pavilion, and with a show of sportsmanship, he slowly pushes the fallen hero over the finishing line as the on-looking crowd erupts in applause.

> **Integrity is immune from robbery and is one of the few things that succeed you at death.**

McQueen may not have won the coveted Piston Cup Championship that day, but what he did win was the conviction of human dignity, and the realization that integrity and sound character mean more than a coveted prize. For too long, society has conditioned us to think that winning requires being the first, the best, the strongest, the fastest, and the brightest. To the contrary, overcomers define victory as the achievement of success against insurmountable odds or arduous difficulties. Overcomers may prefer second place with integrity, versus acquiring first place through deception. Overcomers do the right thing for the right reason even when no one is watching. Overcomers leave a legacy of hard work, persistence, honesty, and integrity long after they are gone. They live with the realization that while it is important to triumph over obstacles, victory is meaningless without integrity. Integrity is immune from robbery and is one of the few things that succeeds you at death. So while some people may narrowly view victory in context of defeat, don't be daunted when you discover that you may not be the fastest person on the track, the smartest person in the room, or considered the best at your craft. Keep pushing forward toward your prize and keep striving toward your goals. While you may suffer setbacks, always remember that victory will meet its companion— integrity—at the finish line of your destiny.

Reflection: *You might not have finished first, or even be the best, the brightest, or the fastest, but victory is yours when you live a life that is ordered by your purpose.*

32.

Blood

WE ARE NOW AT THE final chapter of *Overcomers.* As you reflect on the many lessons that were gleaned within these pages, I trust that you have been inspired to pursue your dreams with passion, purpose, and conviction. In the spirit of Overcomers, I am dedicating this chapter to my Dad—an overcomer who endured a near death experience while this book was being written. Be blessed.

"Six pints of blood now," the surgeon shouted as Dad stretched almost lifeless across the operating table. It is November 21st, 2014, and it's turning out to be quite a busy day already. Over seventeen hundred miles away, my dad is admitted to the hospital to locate the cause for the sudden onset of hemorrhaging. The endoscope is lowered into his upper gastro-intestinal track and everything looks fine. The colonoscopy is next and as soon as the procedure gets under way, blood gushes everywhere. The medical staff scrambles to locate the source of the bleeding, albeit unsuccessfully, and within minutes, what should have been a routine procedure drastically turns into an emergency procedure. With his blood supply deathly low, the surgeon orders "six pints of blood, NOW!" My two siblings frantically begin calling friends in search of donors. The prognosis is grim, and the very real possibility of losing Dad stared us in the face. We needed a miracle, and needed one fast. Across town, my brother and sister are meeting with donors who began to give blood. The telephone rings, and on the other end was a surgeon who saw his friend and patient slipping away. With a strong command, Dr. John exclaimed, "Blood now! Lenard, I need blood now!" Feeling powerless through distance, I interceded for Dad, all the while comforting, encouraging, and reminding my siblings of God's healing power.

It's now after midnight, and it has been a long day for the lab technician. Showing signs of exhaustion, the technician alerts my brother that the lab will be closing and reopening the next day at 7 A.M. All the while my dad's life hung in the balance. Suddenly, a miracle! Lenard remembered the words Dad uttered right before being admitted that included the name of another doctor he knew very well. My brother retrieves the number from Dad's phone and dials the number in search of more blood: "Hello, Dr. Richards, I am Lenard Josiah." Recognizing the lateness of the hour, Dr. Richards replied, "Lennie Josiah, I know, but who are you?" Lenard quickly replies, "I am his first son and he is in dire need of help." Within the hour, Dr. Richards miraculously receives the approval for the emergency release of two pints of blood that were quickly rushed to the operating room. Shortly, thereafter, and with a look of relief, Dr. John emerged. "It's over. Your dad's colectomy was completed in record time!"

Today, Dad is an overcomer since he overcame this near death experience by partnering with the God of life who granted him a second chance at life. He overcame sickness by partnering with a surgeon who was skilled in his field. He overcame with the love and support of a network of family, friends, colleagues, and fellow villagers who love him dearly. The truth is overcomers sometimes do get weak. Overcomers also are incapable of controlling all of life's daunting body blows. In these times, overcomers must not be afraid to reach out and tag team with others who stand ready to lend a helping hand in their time of need. In times of adversity, overcomers turn to their faith, they trust in their God, and they rely in the hope that assures their deliverance. While others may not have been this lucky, Dad now has a new lease on life. Tomorrow may be your turn, and when it does come, know that you too can overcome untimely sickness. Today, place your trust in the God who gives life when all hope is lost. Surround yourself with people who are willing to lend a helping hand. Like overcomers, trust God in every circumstance, knowing that He is the author and finisher of your faith. Trust Him, today, and watch how He turns your mourning into dancing. Trust Him to make you into an overcomer!

33.

Ending

WE DID IT! CONGRATULATIONS ON completing this thirty-one day journey with me. I hope you found this journey informative, challenging, and rewarding. I also hope you will continue reflecting on each of these chapters in the months and years ahead, and draw strength, encouragement, and motivation for your own journey.

Life may be filled with obstacles, but you are now equipped with the tools to overcome them. Life is also brimming with opportunities just for you. I challenge you to use these tools to go after those opportunities and acquire them. Always keep in mind that your life is yours to live and it's really up to you to make the best of it. You decide! I challenge you to never live your life the same. Be the best YOU. Achieve all you can, for in the end, it's YOU who will benefit. Pursue again the dreams that have gone dormant, remembering that you will never reach your full potential building someone else's dreams. Your dreams are your own, and your destiny is yours to reach. In the process, you might sometimes go through difficulty, but hang in there! This is all a part of the journey! In the event you encounter failure along the way, always remember that failure does not define you; rather, failure is an opportunity God chooses to use to refine you. Failure is not, and never will be, a state that defines you. I challenge you to shift your perspective and use the temporary setback that failure might impose and create a statement about who you are, and more importantly, whose you are.

Now, let's go! It's your time to pursue your dreams again and to reach for the stars, because in the end your persistence will pay off, connecting you with your purpose, passion, and ultimately your destiny. It's your time, it's your turn, and it's your year to become an overcomer. It's all within your reach. You can do it. The path to your prize is through perseverance, so push through the limits and pursue your dreams.